APOLOGY TO WOMEN

Thus, they in mutual accusation spent
The fruitless hours, but neither self-condemning,
And of thir vain contest appeerd no end.

John Milton

Apology to Women

*Christian images of
the female sex*

Ann Brown

Inter-Varsity Press

INTER-VARSITY PRESS
38 De Montfort Street, Leicester LE1 7GP, England

Unless otherwise stated, Scripture quotations in this publication are from the Holy Bible, New International Version. Copyright © 1973, 1978, 1984 International Bible Society. Published in Great Britain by Hodder and Stoughton Ltd.

First published 1991
Reprinted 1993

British Library Cataloguing in Publication Data
Brown, Ann *1948–*
   Apology to women.
   1. Women – Christian viewpoints
   I. Title
   261.8344

ISBN 0–85110–694–3

Set in Linotronic Baskerville, 10½ on 12 pt
Phototypeset in Great Britain by
Input Typesetting Ltd, London
Printed and bound in Great Britain
by Cox & Wyman Ltd, Reading

Inter-Varsity Press is the book-publishing division of the Universities and Colleges Christian Fellowship (formerly the Inter-Varsity Fellowship), a student movement linking Christian Unions in universities and colleges throughout the United Kingdom and the Republic of Ireland, and a member movement of the International Fellowship of Evangelical Students. For information about local and national activities write to UCCF, 38 De Montfort Street, Leicester LE1 7GP.

Contents

List of illustrations

Acknowledgments

I wish to express my gratitude to my family and friends who have contributed in so many ways to the writing of this book. It would be impossible to mention by name everyone who has been involved. But I am grateful to all those who have suggested reading, lent books, translated articles, collected newspaper cuttings, read draft chapters, given practical help and generously encouraged. I am indebted to the students and staff in the various European movements of the International Fellowship of Evangelical Students who have stimulated my thinking by vigorously debating the issues discussed in this book.

In particular, I wish to thank Patricia Aithie for her invaluable criticisms of the manuscript, and Jo Bramwell of IVP for empathetically employing her editorial skills and for going beyond the call of duty by making the index. Occasionally, I have leaned heavily on the work of Henri Blocher, Stephen B. Clark, Mary J. Evans, Susan T. Foh, Mary Hayter, James B. Hurley, Andrew Kirk, Alan E. Lewis, John A. Phillips, John Stott and Marina Warner. To these writers I owe some of my ideas and my thanks.

Cardiff   *Ann Brown*
September 1990

Why an apology?

LUCAS Cranach's painting of Paradise which hangs in the Kunsthistorisches Museum, Vienna, encapsulates the way the biblical view of man and woman has been misrepresented in Western cultures. The painting tells the story of the first couple as it unfolds against the backdrop of an idyllic garden planted with luscious plants and trees of many shades of green, among which roam exotic birds and animals. In this setting, God creates Adam from the dust, takes Eve from his side, and later passes judgment on them both. God is portrayed as an old man with a flowing white beard and a red cloak. Satan is depicted as a fair-haired female snake, a mirror image of Eve, proffering the forbidden fruit and tempting man and woman into sin.

It is a beautiful picture, rich in religious symbolism, but its charm is deceptive. Its message is insidious, for it leads the observer to conclude that from the beginning man is more closely identified with God, and woman with sin.

The idea that man is more Godlike and woman defective runs like a distinctive thread through the fabric of Western cultures. Images like these in art and literature have profoundly influenced the way we think of God, and of man and woman.

Cranach, like other painters and writers, followed a well-established tradition when he represented Eve as Satan's accomplice, the one who was primarily responsible for the first sin. Genesis does not pass a verdict of greater guilt on Eve, but biblical interpreters are not always able to resist the temptation to embellish the biblical account. The events in the garden have exerted an enormous fascination over the imaginations of commentators.

Fact and fiction have been meshed together to defame the first woman and denigrate the female sex. Interpretations of the Old Testament, and of the apostle Paul's letters, have often been used to reinforce this negative view of woman, while Mary's story has been amplified to make her the antithesis of Eve and far removed from the realm of other women. Interpreters have not only been guilty of embellishing the biblical accounts. They have also edited women out of the story; good women like Deborah, the Old Testament prophet and judge, have been explained away.

Many women are understandably confused. In any

debate about woman's place in the Christian religion the same questions soon surface. Why is the Bible so anti-woman? Is God male? Is woman in God's image? Is Eve more guilty of the first sin? Why does Paul silence women? The present generation is not the first to raise these issues, though they may have been aired more frequently since the 1960s.

This book responds to these questions. Our objective is to disentangle the factual from the fictitious. In doing so, we will challenge some of the misrepresentations and mis-interpretations of biblical teaching which have been handed down from generation to generation as part of the legacy of Western culture.

We begin by a brief assessment of the impact of culture on biblical interpretation and of the difficulty of escaping our male or female bias when we read the Bible. Then we explore the language and imagery used to portray the Godhead in order to establish whether it implies that God is male. We also attempt to peel away the layers of myth and tradition to disclose the facts about the central female characters, Mary and Eve. We move on to examine the position of women in the patriarchal setting of the Old Testament and the way this altered dramatically with the coming of Jesus. Finally, we question the common assumption that the apostle Paul held prejudiced and jaundiced views of women by looking at some of the varying interpretations of his letters.

Lucas Cranach the Elder (1472–1553), *Das Paradies*, Kunst-historisches Museum, Vienna. This detailed picture tells the story of the first three chapters of Genesis. It is rich in religious symbolism: the neighing horse symbolizes lust, the partridge deceit, peacocks pride and bears evil, while the unicorn and stags stand for lost purity and piety. The goat behind the fallen Adam and Eve shows that they are sinners under God's judgment. God is depicted as an old man, and Satan as a golden-haired maiden, a mirror image of Eve.

The book is an apology in both senses of the word. While admitting that the Bible has been wrongfully used to devalue women, it is also an apology in the sense of being an apologia or defence of the Bible. It is written in the conviction that the Bible itself has a positive and liberating view of women. This is most clearly demonstrated in the life and teaching of Christ. The total inclusion of women in Jesus' ministry stands in stark contrast to their exclusion in most cultures. He preached liberation for both sexes. There is no discrimination in salvation.

Almost a hundred years ago Clara Bewick Colby wrote, 'A careful study of the Bible would alter the views of many as to what it teaches about the position of women.'[1] She is right. An open-minded reading of the Bible reveals that it is not exclusively a man's book focusing on men's interests. It is not a man-made text in which men are the heroes and men's religious experience alone is recorded. Biblical interpreters, commentators, and exegetes may have been guilty of bias but there is no double standard in the way men and women relate to God in the Bible itself.

Note

1 C. B. Colby, 'Comments on Genesis', in E. C. Stanton (ed.), *The Woman's Bible* (1895: Polygon, 1985), Part I, p. 37.

CHAPTER ONE

Whose story?

WOMEN often object that they have disappeared from the pages of history; women have no past because men have written the history books. In the case of the Bible this is not true. Women are clearly in evidence from Genesis to Revelation. Their stories are carefully recounted. Women who feature in the biblical narrative are often women of courage, faith and resolve.[1] Occasionally, women come to prominence administering justice, counselling the king, leading the nation.[2] Most importantly, they are numbered among Jesus' closest followers and witnessed his resurrection.

Disturbingly, women have been led to believe that the Bible is another book written by men, about men, for men. Many women, especially those who have heard the story second hand, assume that women are minor characters in the plot and that the Bible is a man's book documenting male supremacy.

The Bible, it is claimed, propounds a negative view of woman. Elizabeth Cady Stanton, editor of *The Woman's Bible*, protested:

> The Bible teaches that woman brought sin and death into the world, that she precipitated the fall

of the race, that she was arraigned before the judge-
ment seat of heaven, tried, condemned and sentenced. Marriage for her was to be a condition of
bondage, maternity a period of suffering and anguish, and in silence and subjection, she was to play
the role of a dependent on man's bounty for all her
material wants, and for all the information she
might desire on the vital questions of the hour, she
was commanded to ask her husband at home. Here
is the Bible position of woman briefly summed up.[3]

Elizabeth Cady Stanton's summary reflects one-sided
interpretations of the Bible more than the Bible itself. But
generations of women, believing this version of the story
to be true, have turned away from Christianity. The Bible
has come to be seen as a dangerous, political book standing
in the way of women's liberation.

The bias of history

How true is the accusation that since theology has been
monopolized by men the interpretation of the Bible has
been weighted in favour of men? Have biblical commentators, exegetes, preachers and teachers presented woman
less favourably as being only partly in God's image, more
guilty of the original sin and sentenced to silence and
submission? There is some truth in all of this, and later
chapters will take up several of the more negative statements about women. But it would be a mistake to think
that the history of biblical interpretation has been unmiti-
gatingly anti-feminist.

Some of the Church Fathers have become notorious for
their denunciations of women. But we have often overlooked the more positive aspects of their teaching. Take
the following example from Tertullian (d. c. 220), well
known for denouncing woman as the 'devil's gateway' and
holding her primarily responsible for the fall. Writing on

the subject of Christian marriage he said:

> What is the tie of two believers with one hope, one
> discipline, one service? They are siblings; they are
> fellow slaves; there is no separation of spirit or flesh.
> They are truly two in one flesh; where there is one
> flesh, there is also one spirit. Together they pray,
> they work, they fast, teaching, exhorting, supporting
> one another.[4]

According to this description mutuality and interdependence are the characteristics of Christian marriage. They are hardly the words of a misogynist. Elsewhere Tertullian encouraged women to exercise spiritual gifts, quoting the example 'of a sister who has been granted gifts of revelation, which she experiences in church during the Sunday services through ecstatic visions of the spirit'.[5]

Often the Fathers encouraged the women in their congregations to greater exertion as Christians. Chrysostom (d. 407) urged women to emulate Junias in Romans 16:7, of whom he said, 'Oh how great is the devotion of this woman that she should be counted worthy of the appellation of apostle.'[6] Women were very active and prominent in the church. The Fathers were extravagant in their praise of ascetic women. Jerome (d. 420), for example, painted a glowing picture of Paula, one of the leading women in the ascetic circle, as the ideal spiritual woman.[7]

Their teaching is often made to appear more one-sided than it actually is. Even the more aggressive, negative statements about women are explicable if we take into account the cultural context in which these men wrote. The Church Fathers were not harsh women-haters. They tended to adopt a dualistic view of the body and soul, and woman was sometimes used as a symbol of the body in relation to the soul, man. This gives the impression that woman was seen as inferior. Virginity was regarded as superior to marriage since it was the means of transcending the body.[8] They were suspicious of sexuality, which led

15

to an ambivalence about women as the source of sexual temptation; hence the emphasis on women veiling themselves and dressing modestly, and the strong statements about immodest women and Eve.

The Reformers, too, gave a double message about women. The double current in their teaching, partly affirming and partly negating women, has led some to conclude that the Reformation represented a 'limited reformation for women'.[9] The Reformers, as we shall see, went beyond the Scriptures in the limitations that they placed on women, but at the same time they represented progress as they swept away some of the more negative and speculative interpretations and emphasized that woman is man's counterpart, companion and associate.[10]

Whatever they said in print, it is worth noticing that the Reformers were much more positive in practice. Luther appears narrowly to stereotype women's roles in print, while his own wife, Katherine von Bora, was involved in numerous activities. She was 'mistress of a household, a hostel, and a hospital'.[11] She bought a farm at Zulsdorf, two days' journey from their home in Wittenberg. It was intended that the farm would provide her with a living if she were widowed. She regularly went to Zulsdorf for three weeks at a time to attend to work on the farm. Luther addressed letters to her: 'the rich Lady at Zulsdorf', 'my dear wife Katherine von Bora, preacher, brewer, gardener, and whatsoever else she may be', and 'to the saintly worrying Lady Katherine Luther, doctor at Zulsdorf and Wittenberg.'[12]

Calvin, too, appears more generous in practice than in some passages of his commentaries. He praised the spirituality of some of the women involved in the Reformation. In a letter to Madame Falais, he wrote that he was imploring God to 'impart his grace to [her], continuing to uphold [her] as a chosen instrument of his glory, even unto the end'.[13] He wrote to Marguerite de Navarre, Queen of France, 'I know the gifts which our Lord has put on you, and how he has engaged you in his service, and has employed you for the advancement of his kingdom.'[14]

The Bible has not just been used *against* women; it has been used to open up new spheres of activity *to* women. During the Wesleyan revival in Britain in the eighteenth century, for example, a number of women operated as evangelists. They had remarkable ministries. Women like Sarah Crosby and Mary Fletcher regularly preached to crowds of between two and three thousand people in ballrooms, coalpits and quarries as well as chapels. Sarah Crosby was habitually on horseback at five in the morning and it is estimated that in 1777 she covered over 900 miles on horseback.[15]

Some women were reluctant to preach at first because they did not want to go beyond the Bible. But the activities of these female preachers were carefully justified from the Bible by Zechariah Taft. Both he and Mary Fletcher argued that in 1 Timothy 2 the apostle was 'not prohibiting women preaching, but prohibiting them doing it in such a way as to "usurp authority" '.[16] 1 Corinthians 14 was not interpreted as a general prohibition to women to keep silent. When Wesley was asked why he encouraged women to preach, he replied, 'Because God owns them in the conversion of sinners, and who am I that I should withstand God?'[17] At different stages in history others have come to a similar conclusion. Hudson Taylor, founder of the China Inland Mission, for example, readily accepted female missionaries. Justifying his position, he wrote in 1895, 'I think that women may do what God has given them the gift for, if they do it in a womanly way.'[18] It may be that during times of revival and missionary expansion the Bible's teaching about women has been interpreted more generously.[19]

His story v. her story

Race, culture, sex, and nationality all colour the way we read the Bible. Almost without knowing it we can use the

Bible for ideological ends, reading into the text what we want to see. On the subject of sexual differentiation, interpretations tend to veer to one of two extremes, either absolutizing the differences between the sexes and making one sex superior, or relativizing and minimizing sexual differentiation.[20]

The New Testament attitude to women is radical, but most cultures have been overwhelmingly male-dominated and the church has found it a formidable task to counter this influence. It has tended to adopt patriarchal thinking and develop interpretations of the Bible which absolutize the differences between the sexes. The Bible has been used to reinforce cultural assumptions about a woman's place. Some of Paul's statements, in particular, have become proof-texts of women's inferiority and man's superiority. Culture has coloured the way the Bible has been read. Slavery, sexism and racism have all been justified by selective reading of the Bible. It is always easier to adopt cultural prejudices than a radical New Testament perspective. The church has not always examined whether its practices are cultural and traditional or thoroughly biblical.

In reaction and protest against male-biased interpretations of the Bible, women have produced their own versions of the story.

Another story

Some women have moved out of the Christian church in search of a religion for women. Believing that God is male and Christianity irredeemably sexist, they have staged their own exodus from the man's church. This group are often called *post-Christian* feminists,[21] though, strictly speaking, 'pre-Christian feminists' is more accurate, because in many cases they find inspiration in the worship of the pre-Christian goddesses who are mentioned in the Old Testament.[22] Christianity is being replaced with a woman-centred, matriarchal religion in which men have no part.

This alternative religion sets up a dualistic world view

in which women are the wronged, men the wrongdoers. Women are the victims. Sexism is seen as the fundamental sin. Salvation comes through women's consciousness. But ultimately this view fails to recognize that man's inhumanity to woman is not the only evil. Even if all forms of male domination could be removed, the alienation between women and within each woman would remain.

Rewriting the story

> I must enter my protest against the false translations, . . . and against the perverted interpretation . . . I am inclined to think that when we are admitted to the honour of studying Greek and Hebrew, we shall produce some various readings of the Bible a little different from those we have now.[23]

Taking their cue from comments like this, Elizabeth Cady Stanton and her revising committee produced *The Woman's Bible* at the end of the nineteenth century. It was a full revision of the Bible from a woman's point of view. They adopted a 'scissors and paste' method of working. Each person marked all the texts referring to women, cut the passages out and pasted them in a book, so that commentaries could be written underneath.

Since then many feminist theologians have adopted this *revisionist* approach. Beginning with the assumption that the Bible would have been different if it had been written by a woman, they have set about rewriting and reinterpreting it. Unlike the post-Christian feminists, the revisionists do not reject the Bible completely; they believe there are redeemable, liberating elements within the text. They aim to liberate the Bible from patriarchy. They focus on this liberating tradition, which becomes the canon within the canon.[24] The key to interpreting the Bible is *woman's experience*.[25] Her version of the story is opposed to his version.

The problem with this approach is that women's

experience becomes the measure of all things. It becomes the absolute by which everything else is judged. What is true for women becomes truth.

Re-reading the story

A third group of theologians, some of whom would call themselves *biblical feminists*, do not believe that the Bible itself is oppressive or misogynist but they do take issue with some of the ways in which it has been interpreted. By careful exegesis, or by consideration of the cultural context, they attempt to redress the balance. Their contention is that the Bible is not a book written by men for men, but that it has often been interpreted by men for men. Without writing a new version of the story, they insist that the Bible is a woman's book. Fundamental to this perspective is the conviction that the Bible is God's Word, not merely men's words.[26]

Unbiased interpretation

This book is written with the conviction that the Bible is not a man-made message; it is God's message through which he speaks and reveals himself to an alienated humanity. Since it is the voice of God, the Bible as a whole is uniquely authoritative.[27]

On the issue of men's and women's roles, however, it is particularly difficult to get out of our own skins and escape our male or female bias when we read the Bible. All too easily, biblical interpretation becomes part of gender warfare. Without being aware of it, we can subtly weight the evidence against the opposite sex and develop a 'them against us' interpretation of the Bible. Perhaps the test of whether we are really listening to the Bible is whether our ideological presuppositions are being challenged.[28] The Bible should make us feel uncomfortable. We may not always find in it the answers that we want to find.

Is it possible to interpret the Bible in an unbiased way? Three cardinal principles are to read a passage bearing in mind its *literary form*, its *context* both immediate and within the whole Bible, and the *historical setting* in which it was written.[29] Let me briefly explain.

First, the Bible includes many different types of *literary genre*. It is important to understand whether a passage is poetry, historical narrative, prose, or wisdom literature. Is it psalm or prophecy? Is it law or letter? Grammatical structure, figures of speech, idioms, parables, analogies, images and metaphors all have to be read in the appropriate way. The Samaritan woman, whose conversation with Jesus is recorded by John, misunderstood him when he offered her 'living water' because she took his words literally rather than figuratively when he spoke metaphorically of eternal life. 'You have nothing to draw with and the well is deep', she replied. 'Where can you get this living water?' (Jn. 4:11).

Careful attention must be given, secondly, to the *context of a passage*. This is particularly important in the apostle Paul's letters where the arguments are often complex. Simone de Beauvoir in *The Second Sex* creates the impression that the apostle Paul was savagely anti-feminist by lifting several of his statements about women out of context.[30] She quotes Paul's words, 'For man did not come from woman, but woman from man; neither was man created for woman, but woman for man' (1 Cor. 11:8). She regards this as a value judgment on woman and does not take into account that this sentence is part of an intricate argument. Two sentences later Paul balances what he said earlier by adding, 'In the Lord, however, woman is not independent of man, nor is man independent of woman. For as woman came from man, so also man is born of woman. But everything comes from God' (1 Cor. 11:11–12).

Generally, a Bible passage should be read in the context of the whole of Scripture, the unclear in the context of the clear; though even with cross-reference, comparison and reconciling of texts, some question-marks may remain.[31] It is a mistake to make absolute what is not clearly absolute in Scripture.

Thirdly, an awareness of the *cultural, historical, and geographical background* to a biblical passage often heightens its significance. The conversation between Jesus the Jewish rabbi and the Samaritan woman, for example, may seem no more than an everyday occurrence to the reader unaware of the first-century conflict between the Jews and the Samaritans. Samaria consisted of the northern part of Israel, between Judea and Galilee. The Samaritans had built their own temple on Mount Gerizim; there was fierce rivalry between the two groups. In fact, relations between Jews and Samaritans were so poor in the time of Jesus that most Jews would have avoided travelling through Samaria. But, on the occasion that John records, Jesus took the route from Judea to Galilee which passed through Samaria. As he sat by Jacob's well a Samaritan woman came to draw water. Jesus asked her for a drink (Jn. 4:1–26). Seen in its historical context Jesus' behaviour was startling and radical.

An appreciation of the cultural background may also influence the way the Bible is applied to contemporary situations. It is exciting that a book written so long ago still speaks into our lives today. At the same time the Bible reflects the different cultural settings in which it was written and these are far removed from our own contemporary cultures.

Obedience to God's Word does not mean copying all the customs of the ancient world. Jesus washed the disciples' feet and commanded his followers to do likewise (Jn. 13:12–17). In many countries today it is not customary to extend a welcome by washing guests' feet. Christians obey Christ's command by serving one another in ways that are appropriate in contemporary culture.

As we read the Bible we have to distinguish between the revelation of God's truth, which is timeless and unchanging, and the cultural application of that truth, which may change. In 1 Corinthians 11, for example, Paul writes about sexual differentiation being ordained in creation, and as a reflection of the relationships within the Trinity this is clearly transcultural and unchanging. He then goes on to discuss a cultural practice which may refer to the veiling of women or the way women wore their hair. It would be difficult for contemporary women to imitate this custom because we cannot be sure what it was. In obedience to this passage many churches have adopted a head-covering policy for women. But does wearing a hat or head-covering in church have the same significance today as wearing a veil had in Corinth? The way to apply the principle today may be to resist cultural practices which blur sexual distinctions (for instance, cross-dressing or gender-bending fashions).

Interpreters who absolutize the differences between the sexes also tend to absolutize the customs of the biblical world regarding men and women. Those who relativize sexual differentiation also tend to dismiss biblical teaching as being culturally relative. An alternative approach is to accept biblical teaching as authoritative but to translate it into appropriate contemporary cultural expressions. 'It is essential to recognise that the purpose of "cultural transposition" (the practice of transposing the teaching of Scripture from one culture into another) is not to avoid obedience but rather to ensure it, by making it contemporary.'[32]

Even though interpreters may adhere to the same principles of interpretation, they do not necessarily come up with exactly the same answers. Some of the more difficult New Testament passages, in particular, allow for several interpretations. We may not reach unanimity on every point, but I believe that anyone who reads the Bible in an unprejudiced way would have to agree that it has as much relevance to women as to men. The Bible was not written exclusively for men. In the sweep of biblical history, beginning with creation and the rupture with God in Eden, through the gradual unfolding of God's plan of salvation for humanity, women are included at every stage. There is no need to rewrite the story, though we may need to reread it more carefully. The Bible's message of liberation is for women too. The Godhead, as we shall see in the next chapter, relates to women as directly as to men.

Notes

1 Ex. 1:15–20; Jos. 2; 1 Sa. 1; 25:3–42.

2 Jdg. 4; 2 Ki. 22:14–20; Mi. 6:4.

3 E. C. Stanton (ed.), *The Woman's Bible* (1895: Polygon, 1985), Part I, p. 7.

4 Tertullian, *Ad uxorem* 11, 9, quoted in S. B. Clark, *Man and Woman in Christ* (Servant Books, 1980), p. 290.

5 Tertullian, *De anima* IX, *Ante-Nicene Christian Library*, vol. 11 (T. and T. Clark, 1870).

6 *The Homilies of St John Chrysostom*, vol. 11, quoted in M. J. Evans, *Woman in the Bible* (Paternoster, 1983), p. 124.

7 Jerome, *Ep.* 108. For a discussion see R. R. Ruether, 'Mysogynism and Virginal Feminism in the Fathers of the Church', in R. R. Ruether (ed.), *Religion and Sexism* (Simon and Schuster, 1974), pp. 172–3.

8 For a discussion of patristic theology see Clark, *Man and Woman*, pp. 281–327; and R. R. Ruether (ed.), *Religion and Sexism*, pp. 150–83.

9 M. Potter explores this idea in 'Gender Equality and Gender Hierarchy in Calvin's Theology', *Signs: Journal of Women in Culture and Society*, vol. II, no. 4.

10 *E.g.* J. Calvin, *Commentary on Genesis* (Banner of Truth, 1975), pp. 130–1.

11 R. Bainton, *Women of the Reformation*, vol. 1, *In Germany and Italy* (Augsburg, 1971), p. 30.

12 Bainton, *Women of the Reformation*, pp. 39–40.

13 Quoted in Potter, 'Gender Equality'.

14 Quoted in Potter, 'Gender Equality'.

15 G. Willis, unpublished and incomplete M. Th. thesis for the University of Wales, Bangor, pp. 16, 33.

16 Willis, p. 46.

17 Willis, p. 7.

18 Quoted by M. Langley, *Equal Woman: A Christian Feminist Perspective* (Marshall, Morgan and Scott, 1983), p. 82.

19 M. Langley argues that this is the case in *Equal Woman*, p. 83.

20 H. Blocher, *In the Beginning* (IVP, 1984), p. 101, argues that there has been a tendency among secular thinkers either to absolutize or to minimize sexual differentiation.

21 *E.g.* M. Daly, *Beyond God the Father* (Beacon Press, 1973).

22 A. Kirk coins this term in 'Theology from a Feminist Perspective', in K. Keay (ed.), *Men, Women and God* (Marshall Pickering, 1987), p. 27.

23 Sarah Grimké (1838), quoted in D. Spender, *Women of Ideas (and What Men have Done to Them)* (Ark, 1982), pp. 221–2.

24 Among this revisionist group are Elisabeth Schussler Fiorenza, Rosemary Radford Ruether, Letty M. Russell and Phyllis Trible. Trible explains how Ruether and Fiorenza select their canons in 'Postscript: Jottings on the Journey', in L. M. Russell (ed.), *Feminist Interpretation of the Bible* (Basil Blackwell, 1985), pp. 148–9.

25 For a discussion of women's experience as a critical force in hermeneutics see R. R. Ruether, 'A Method of Correlation', in Russell (ed.), *Feminist Interpretation*, pp. 111–2.

26 Among this group are Paul Jewett, Myrtle Langley, Virginia Ramey Mollenkott, Letha Scanzoni and Nancy Hardesty, who tend to employ a hermeneutic of deculturization. Others, such as Mary J. Evans, *Woman in the Bible* (Paternoster, 1983), re-examine the biblical material but emphasize careful exegesis rather than the cultural conditioning of the Bible.

27 Biblical writers claimed to be authorized by God, and recognized each other's authority. Most importantly, Jesus endorsed the authority of the Old Testament, and authorized the apostles, whose teaching makes up the New Testament, to teach in his name. Jesus' claims about his own authority and the authority of the Bible must, therefore, be assessed together. For a longer discussion see J. Stott, *Understanding the Bible* (Scripture Union, 1972), pp. 137–56.

28 W. M. Swartley, *Slavery, Sabbath, War and Women* (Herald Press, 1983), pp. 183–4, develops this point.

29 For a longer discussion of the interpretation of the Bible see Stott, *Understanding the Bible*, pp. 156–83.

30 S. de Beauvoir, *The Second Sex* (1949: Penguin, 1972), pp. 128–9.

31 For a longer discussion see Kirk, 'Feminine perspective', in Keay (ed.), *Men, Women and God*, pp. 38ff.

32 Stott, *Understanding the Bible*, p. 175.

CHAPTER TWO

Is God male?

The God I been praying and writing to is a man. And act just like all the other mens I know. Trifling, forgitful and lowdown. . . . He big and old and tall and graybearded and white. He wear white robes and go barefooted. . . . I'm still adrift. Trying to chase that old white man out of my head.[1]

CELIE'S letter to Nettie in *The Color Purple* would have been unusual thirty years ago. But increasingly women with a raised consciousness are objecting to the fact that the Judaeo-Christian God is apparently male. In Christian worship God is addressed as Father; Jesus came to earth as a man and is called the Son. In the Bible, God is described as a king, husband, shepherd. This chapter examines this masculine language and imagery. Does it all mean that God is male?

This has become a crucial issue. In part, it is rooted in the very real fear that Christianity is idolatry of the male. Some feminists protest that if God is male, females automatically become the second sex. Women who have come to this conclusion have often decided that there is no place for them in the Christian church.

It is also related to the feminist conviction that all

linguistic discrimination in and out of the church must be removed. Feminist theory argues that man-made language is used to control, exclude and alienate women; it must, therefore, be censored.[2] Women who have become aware of their exclusion from the language of Zion have taken initiatives in revising prayer books, hymn books and the Bible to produce non-sexist, inclusive-language versions.[3] Not only are masculine words being replaced by inclusive terms (such as 'sisters and brothers' for 'brethren'), but the use of inclusive language is extended to the Godhead. So, for example, 'God the Father' may be translated as 'God the Father and Mother', 'Son of God' as 'Child of God', and 'Son of Man' as 'the Human One'.[4] The way God is addressed has become ideologically significant.

A man-made God?

Behind the objection to the use of masculine terminology for God often lurks the suspicion that God is after all man-made. Central to the debate about the gender of God is the question, 'Is God in man's image or is man in God's image?' Dale Spender, the Australian feminist writer, states as one of her articles of faith, 'Man made God in his own image and not the other way around.'[5] In this way the women's movement has appropriated the psychological theory of projection from Feuerbach and Freud. The Christian God is, therefore, rejected as being a projection of male ideas and ideals, created by men because they need him. Men dream of being self-sufficient, autonomous and omnipotent, so they have created God to correspond to this deep-seated fantasy.[6] From this perspective, men have created a male God and a religion which has their own interests at heart. God, it is argued, has been enlisted on the side of men. As the projection of the patriarchal head of the family, he is used to legitimize the oppression of women.

The idea that those in need of God have invented him

to meet their needs is a familiar objection to Christianity. It is one of those chicken-and-egg objections that soon have everyone tied in knots. Which comes first, the need for God, or God? Basically, we are faced with two alternative propositions:

1. Man needs God; man creates God.
2. God created man; man needs God.

Psychological studies of religious experience may help to explain why and how individuals embrace the second proposition and reject the first, but they shed no light on which proposition is true. The fact that Christianity is subjectively satisfying does not necessarily prove that God is man's creation. Just the opposite may be true. We can turn the argument on its head to argue that men and women, as God's creatures made in his image, discover their greatest satisfaction in relationship with him. As Augustine put it, 'Our hearts are restless till they rest in thee.' We must not confuse psychology with epistemology. Questions of truth belong to epistemology, not to the domain of psychology.[7]

I find it hard to believe that anyone who has open-mindedly examined God's self-revelation in the Bible, in particular in the person of Jesus Christ, can seriously allege that God is a projection. The fullness of God's character is so beyond our imaginations, it is inconceivable that he is the product of finite minds. From whatever angle we care to look at Jesus' life as recorded in the gospels, he is above reproach and bears out his own claim to be God. If we look at him from the point of view of women, we discover that Jesus' behaviour as God in the flesh is so distinctive in its freedom from any hint of sexism that it is impossible to believe that he has been fabricated by men's minds in the first century. The God who is revealed in the Bible is obviously not just on man's side, or there to meet man's needs. God is not a masculine idea; he is not a figment of the male imagination. We do not have to read far into the Bible to see that God sometimes opposes men and judges them for their stubborn pride and disobedience. If men had created God, surely they would have made him a little more indulgent, and willing to turn a blind eye to their failings.

Interestingly, the Bible specifically repudiates the theory of projection in that we are told not to make images of God in our own likeness. The second commandment makes this explicit (Ex. 20:4). Throughout the Old Testament God is contrasted with man-made idols, the creations of men's hands and minds (*e.g.* Is. 44). Apparently, the theory of projection had already been voiced about 1000 BC, since the prophet Isaiah rebutted it by saying:

> You turn things upside down,
>   as if the potter were thought to be like the clay!
> Shall what is formed say to him who formed it,
>   'He did not make me'?
> Can the pot say of the potter,
>   'He knows nothing'? (Is. 29:16)

The theory of projection cannot explain away God, but it may help us to understand the way we pin false images and caricatures on to God. We can slip into believing in our own limited picture of God rather than the biblical description of God. This is very pertinent to the discussion of God's gender. The Bible, as we will see in the next section, avoids any suggestion that God is sexual, yet we easily project human sexuality on to the Godhead. The image of God that we assimilate from our Western culture is undoubtedly male. Whenever the clouds open in paintings of the creation, annunciation, nativity and crucifixion, God is almost always portrayed in male form. In this sense, God has been *re*made in man's image.

Beyond gender

Many women feel alienated and cut off from this male God. When God is depicted as being more like one sex than the other, a power struggle inevitably ensues. As a reaction to the over-masculinization of God, one strand of religious feminism interprets the Old Testament as a battle between the male God of the Jews and other male and female deities. The Bible is reinterpreted and made to fit into the framework of other ancient Near Eastern cultures in which it is common to find hostilities between male and female gods.[8]

It is true that the Old Testament writers denounced in extremely strong language the fertility cults and the veneration of female deities.[9] But it is important to understand that they were not motivated by antipathy to women. Their aim was not to replace these goddesses with a male god. In fact, they condemned the Baals and other male gods as vehemently as the goddesses. Their purpose was to establish that Yahweh is unique and has nothing in common with the pantheon of male and female deities of the fertility religions.[10] Unlike the fertility cults which attributed male or female sexuality to their deities, the prophets emphasized God's transcendence. God is maker, creator, saviour, redeemer, Holy One.[11]

The Old Testament prophets commanded an exclusive allegiance to Yahweh,[12] and abhorred the sexual rites of the fertility religions.[13] These rites were designed to ensure good harvests and fruitfulness by re-enacting the divine sexual activity.[14] The cycles of nature were believed to be the perennial mating and procreating of these divine couples. The Old Testament view of God is radically different. Unlike the pantheistic fertility gods, God stands quite apart from creation. An emphasis on the sexuality of gods and goddesses belongs to the nature religions, not to Christianity.

Both those who represent God as a harsh, power-loving patriarch and those who concentrate exclusively on the sympathetic, approachable, maternal side of God distort the biblical characterization of God. The Judaeo-Christian God is above sexual categories and sexual differentiation. Sexuality is a characteristic of God's creatures but not of the Creator. God as spirit is neither male nor female, but is beyond gender, or genderless. In fact, to ask whether God is physically male or female is a nonsense question; it is like asking whether the wind is red or blue. The Bible insists that God is not to be depicted by making male or female figures. Deuteronomy gives a strong warning:

> You saw no form of any kind the day the Lord spoke to you at Horeb out of the fire. Therefore watch yourselves very carefully, so that you do not become corrupt and make for yourselves an idol, an image of any shape, whether formed like a man or a woman. (Dt. 4:15–16)

In the same way, in the New Testament the apostle Paul condemned the folly of those who 'exchanged the glory of the immortal God for images made to look like mortal man' (Rom. 1:23). Neither sex is to make God in its own image. Yet the tendency remains to picture male or female when we think of God. Interestingly, the command in Deuteronomy is prefaced by a reminder that at Horeb they saw no form. In their descriptions of their encounters with God the prophets never give a clear visual impression of God. But they emphasize his character, especially his holiness.

At the same time man and woman are made in God's image. In the image of God 'male and female he created them' (Gn. 1:27). At the deepest level man and woman do resemble God. But this does not mean that God is male, female or bisexual. God embraces and transcends male and female.

The Father

God is not sexual, but he is personal. This is where the confusion arises, for we automatically associate sexuality with personality. The Bible is full of personal language about God. We learn what it means to have a personal relationship with God through analogies. Four analogies

31

are most commonly employed: God is depicted as a king, husband, shepherd, and father. This is the crux of the problem because they are all male analogies.

But we must not be over-literal in the way we understand these analogies. In an analogy, the unfamiliar (for example, how God relates to his people) is compared with the familiar (for example, a shepherd's relationship to his sheep). But the comparison is not an exact one. When we read Psalm 23, beginning 'The Lord is my Shepherd . . . ', we understand immediately that we are not meant to think of God literally as a shepherd with crook in hand and sheep-dog at heel, nor are we to think of ourselves literally as sheep. A children's paraphrase of this psalm imagines a small child grinning and saying to himself, 'I don't eat grass. And I don't drink from quiet pools the way sheep do.'[15] A child can grasp the limitations of the shepherd/sheep analogy. In the same way, to say God is our Father does not imply that he shares the physical characteristics of human fathers.[16]

At the same time, the fatherhood of God is more than an analogy. God is not just like a father, as in the parable of the prodigal son, but he actually *is* our Father, if we are Christians. What does this mean? Jesus came to show us the Father. As theologian Tom Smail puts it: 'We have to live in the light of Jesus' revelation of God and not in the darkness of our own caricatures.'[17] To say that God is our Father to someone who has experienced nothing but rejection or cruelty at the hands of a father may sound like a sick joke. How can such a person ever form a positive view of God? One woman who had a very damaging relationship with her father provides the key. She recalls that when she first became a Christian she found it impossible to pray to God as Father. But then she saw that 'our heavenly Father is just so different'.

Jesus' revelation of God the Father forces people to think again, whatever negative connotations the word 'father' may have for them. In the gospels he paints a picture of perfect fatherliness; of a heavenly Father who knows and responds to his children's needs, is always available, sets limits and loves unconditionally.[18] No wonder Jesus told his followers to pray to 'Abba' ('Daddy', 'Papa'). He named God in a way that was completely revolutionary in its familiarity and intimacy. In Judaism God is never addressed as Father; Jesus did the unthinkable when he prayed to God as Abba. To use an everyday children's word must have sounded extremely disrespectful to the ears of his first-century hearers. His contemporaries were deeply offended; on several occasions they tried to stone him because he dared to call God his Father and commanded his followers to do the same.

In his prayers Jesus habitually spoke to God as Abba. This is a unique way of addressing God 'that expresses the heart of Jesus' relationship to God'.[19] He commands his followers to pray in the same way. They are adopted into a wonderful new family relationship in which they may have to relearn the meaning of the word 'father'. John is at pains to explain that adoption into this family depends on spiritual rebirth, not on a sexual act. In the prologue to his gospel he writes, 'Yet to all who received him, to those who believed in his name, he gave the right to become children of God – children born not of natural descent, nor of human decision or a husband's will, but born of God' (Jn. 1:12–13).

The way God was named by Jesus does not mean that he has dramatically changed character between the Old and New Testaments. On some occasions in the Old Testament, God is compared to a father, but he is never addressed as Father. For example, God is portrayed as a father who guides, cares for and has compassion on his children.[20] The object of these comparisons is never to make the point that God is male, but to emphasize some aspect of God's character and the way he relates to his people.

Jesus recognized that our idea of fatherhood is limited by our own earthly experience. He was careful to stress that God far transcends human fatherhood. In the context of teaching about prayer, he said that if even evil men respond to their children's requests for food, 'how much more will your Father in heaven give good gifts to those who ask him?' (Mt. 7:11). Compare the best of human fathers with God and we still have to say 'how much more' of our Father in heaven. God is not a projection of human fatherhood. We must measure fathers on earth against our Father in heaven, and not the other way around.

The motherhood of God debate

The Church of Scotland had a rude awakening at the 1982 Annual General Meeting of the Women's Guild, when Anne Hepburn, the National President, prayed to 'God our Mother', and 'Dear Mother God'. The prayer provoked intense reactions, both positive and negative. But the motherhood of God debate is by no means restricted to the northern kirk; reverberations are being felt throughout all Western cultures. Not only the language but also the symbols of Christianity are being feminized or androgynized. In April 1984 the Episcopalian Cathedral of St John the Divine in New York became newsworthy when it displayed Edwina Sandys' bronze of a female figure on a cross.

Those who favour a maternal approach to God point to certain passages of the Bible and to Christians throughout the history of Christianity who have set the precedent in their devotions by praying to and meditating on God as Mother. They come from different church traditions, including Greek and Russian Orthodox, Roman Catholic and Protestant. Early examples are Clement of Alexandria (third century), Augustine of Hippo (fourth century), and Gregory of Nyssa (fourth century). There are numerous examples in the medieval period; among the most notable are Anselm of Canterbury (eleventh century), Bernard of Clairvaux (twelfth century), Birgitta of Sweden and Julian of Norwich (fourteenth century), and later Count von Zinzendorf (eighteenth century).

Recurring themes in their writings are new-birth and

breast-feeding images. So, for example, Augustine wrote: 'What am I but a creature suckled on your milk and feeding on yourself, the food that never perishes.'[21]

Anselm of Canterbury, in his prayer to St Paul, meditated on the motherly qualities of Jesus Christ as demonstrated in his saving work:

> And you Jesus, are you not also a mother? Are you not the mother who, like a hen, gathers her chicks under her wings? Truly, Lord, you are a mother; for both they who are in labour and they who are brought forth are accepted by you. For, longing to bear sons into life, you tasted of death, and by dying, you begot them. You did this in your own self, your servants by your commands and help. You as the author, they as the ministers. So you, Lord God, are the great mother.[22]

Julian of Norwich provides a developed treatment of God's motherhood in her *Revelations of Divine Love*. A major theme in her writing, too, is that we are reborn through the second person of the Trinity. She wrote:

> In Jesus, our true Mother, has our life been grounded through his own uncreated foresight, and the Father's almighty power ... In taking our nature he restored us to life; and now ... he feeds and helps us on ... just as one would expect the supreme and royal nature of motherhood to act, and the natural needs of children to require. Beautiful and sweet is our heavenly Mother in the sight of our souls; and, in the sight of our heavenly Mother, dear and lovely are the gracious children ... There is no higher state in this life than that of childhood, because of our inadequate and feeble capacity and intellect, until such time as our gracious Mother shall bring us up to our Father's bliss.[23]

Count Zinzendorf, the Moravian pietist, writing much later, considered the Spirit to be our Mother. He described the Trinity in these terms: 'The Father of our Lord Jesus Christ is our true Father, the Spirit of our Lord Jesus Christ is our true Mother, because the Son of the living God is our true brother.'[24]

What is interesting is that these writers do not appear to contemplate motherhood in opposition to, or to the exclusion of, the fatherhood of God. The maternal imagery forms part of their personal devotional lives and is not used in an ideological way.

It was not until the nineteenth century that Elizabeth Cady Stanton and the women who worked with her to produce *The Woman's Bible* articulated the ideological significance of addressing God as Mother. She argued that 'the first step in the elevation' of woman is the recognition 'of an ideal Heavenly Mother, to whom prayers should be addressed, as well as a Father'.[25]

In 1888, Matilda Joslyn Gage, the foremother of radical feminist theologians, put this injunction into practice when she opened a session at the International Council of Women with a prayer to a female deity.[26] Since the publication of *The Woman's Bible* the masculine language used to describe God has been regarded as yet another device to keep women in their place.

Biblical feminists, however, attempt by careful exegesis to give fuller appreciation to the neglected passages of maternal imagery without abandoning the Father, and without implying that God is sexual.[27] They emphasize that as well as the male imagery that is used to describe God, the Bible includes some explicitly maternal imagery. Some of this female imagery is derived from the animal world. God is likened to a protective mother eagle bearing up the eaglets on her wings, and to an angry she-bear who has been deprived of her cubs.[28]

God is depicted as mothering and being motherly. In some poignant and beautiful passages, God is compared to a woman crying out, gasping and panting in childbirth, and to a mother nursing, quieting and consoling a child.[29] These are remarkable and powerful images. The breast-feeding image graphically illustrates the strength and warmth of the relationship between God and his children: ' . . . a baby feeding at the breast, or sleeping on the breast, full, satisfied and loved. This picture, so rich and evocative of maternal love, is a wonderful image of God's care for us; the breast unites food, warmth and intimacy with the giver of our life.'[30]

In the New Testament, too, God is compared to a woman. In the parable of the woman and the lost coin Jesus portrayed God as a woman who has lost one of her ten silver coins and searches carefully until she finds it (Lk. 15:8–10).

This female imagery is striking because it explodes the myth that only male imagery can be used to describe God. God is not a man's God. He is not the product of men's minds or the projection of male ideals. Male standards and activities have not become sacred. For if this were the case, how did the female imagery creep into the text?

At the same time, these passages of female imagery do not make God female any more than the male analogies make God male. Imagery is only imagery. It can help us to understand God's character and our relationship to God, but it does not make God literally male or female. God is not limited or defined by the imagery.[31] In fact, God far transcends the imagery. God possesses motherly qualities, but to a degree not found in human mothers. God's love surpasses comparison with a mother's love. As one French pastor remarked in a Mother's Day sermon, 'All the mothers in the world put together reflect only in part the limitless love of God.'[32]

Generally, the maternal side of God has been neglected or underplayed. This may be because of the difficulty of knowing how to incorporate maternal references to God into worship, or because the passages of maternal imagery are relatively few in number. Whatever the reason, many women lament this sad neglect, and some argue that the time has come to address God as Mother. This raises a host of questions. Does it follow that because both paternal and maternal language is used of God, we may pray to our Father and/or Mother? Are the two titles complementary and interchangeable? Does 'Mother', which has been repressed for so long, offer a fresh and more meaningful approach today? Has 'Father' become a worn metaphor which has lost its original impact?[33]

There are in fact some important differences between the ways in which paternal and maternal comparisons are used in the Bible. In the maternal imagery, various actions or attributes of God are compared to those of mothers. For example, God comforts his people as a mother comforts her child (Is. 66:13). However, God is never actually addressed as Mother.[34] But Jesus did command us to pray to our Father, and in his personal prayers he prayed exclusively to God as Father.

But can we ignore the precedent set by Jesus? Virginia Ramey Mollenkott argues that we can. According to her, it was for cultural reasons that Jesus did not command us to pray to God as Mother. She argues that he would have been misunderstood, and that, had he prayed to our Mother, it would have been mistaken for some kind of pantheism.[35] This is not very convincing. Jesus was misunderstood for most of his ministry, but he taught regardless of the opposition that he created. Repeatedly, he challenged the mores of his first-century culture. Jesus caused cultural shockwaves by calling God his Father. If he had wanted to pray to God as Mother, cultural considerations alone would not have prevented him.

It is important to see the implications of addressing God as Mother. Many of those who are battling against limited, male pictures of God have understandably opted for praying to God as Mother. But this is really no answer at all. The disturbing fact is that addressing God as Mother–Father encourages the idea that God is sexual. Adding Mother to Father gives the impression that 'divine maleness must be supplemented by divine femaleness or replaced by divine androgyny'.[36] This completely changes the biblical view of God as non-sexual and beyond gender.

To change the way that we address God is ultimately to talk about a different god. Some feminist theologians are determined to change gods. Revisionists reject any biblical language, including the fatherhood of God, that smacks of patriarchy. They use the Bible selectively, extracting the non-patriarchal elements, and rewriting and reinterpreting it to produce an alternative religious language and theology.[37] Rosemary Radford Reuther insists that it is not enough to change words and speak of Mother as opposed to Father, but that the whole concept of God must change. She replaces God with the symbol 'God/ess'. 'God/ess' is defined as the 'primal Matrix, the ground of being – new being'. It is 'neither stifling immanence nor rootless transcendence; spirit and matter are not dichotomized but are the inside and the outside of the same thing.'[38] Many of the revisionist reinterpretations, like Rosemary Radford Ruether's, are coloured by the thinking of theologians like Tillich. They conceive of God in mystical, pantheistic terms, beyond personality. God becomes distant, impersonal, unknowable. Prayer is replaced by meditation. Such reformulations are very different from the God whose self-revelation we have in the Bible.

From the biblical perspective, we are not free to address God as we see fit, or to create slogans to fit in with our own particular ideology. Jill Tweedie, who describes herself as an enquiring atheist, comments on the current trend of feminizing God: 'Recently, we have shown a little audacity. We have drawn cartoons of a man running out of a stable and shouting "It's a girl." Worth a giggle but the laughter springs from nervousness at blasphemy against God.'[39]

It takes someone outside the church to recognize that the word-games we are playing in church are perilously close to blasphemy. 'So what's in a name?' you may ask. The mentality of the Bible is that a name is not just a label. The name represents the person to whom it belongs. The name is intrinsic to the person. In the Old Testament the Jews held the Lord's name in such reverence that they hardly dared to take it upon their lips. Jesus told his disciples to pray to 'Abba', 'Daddy', 'Papa', but followed it with 'Hallowed be your name' (Mt. 6:9). Jesus regarded 'Abba' as a sacred form of address. He commanded the disciples, 'Do not call anyone on earth "father", for you have one Father and he is in heaven' (Mt. 23:9). He was referring to the practice of addressing older, distinguished members of the community as father. He forbade this custom. 'Abba' is to be reserved for addressing God. This indicates the extent to which Jesus felt the word 'Abba' should be held in esteem.[40] We desperately need to recapture this understanding of God.

The Son

What are we to make of the fact that when Jesus became incarnate, he was a man? Does this suggest a certain bias in the Godhead? Within some church traditions Christ's maleness has been taken to imply that only a man can properly represent him in what are seen as priestly or sacramental functions.[41] Hardly surprisingly, some of the most negative reactions to Jesus come from women within these traditions.[42]

Others try to feminize Jesus. For example, the female figure of Wisdom in the Old Testament (Pr. 8:22–31) is identified with the pre-existent Christ, similar to the pre-existent Word.[43] The figure of Wisdom is closely linked with God, but it seems more likely that Wisdom personifies an attribute of God rather than being the pre-existent Christ.[44] It may be that wisdom became flesh in Jesus, but this is not explicit in the New Testament. Jesus is described as having the Spirit of wisdom, being 'filled with wisdom' and becoming 'for us Wisdom from God'.[45] But Jesus himself personifies wisdom in his teaching without identifying himself as the figure of Wisdom.[46] The picture of Wisdom as a female figure tells us nothing about the gender of the second person of the Trinity.

There is just one occasion when Jesus described himself in a maternal way:

> O Jerusalem, Jerusalem, you who kill the prophets and stone those sent to you, how often I have longed to gather your children together, as a hen gathers her chicks under her wings, but you were not willing. (Mt. 23:37)

The reference is similar to the passages of maternal imagery in the Old Testament in which God is compared to a mother. The comparison that Jesus made in Matthew evokes beautifully the depth of his protective yearning for his people and the unnaturalness of their rejection, but it by no means makes him female.

There is no escaping the fact that Jesus came to earth as a man. But biblical feminists put this in its biblical perspective by showing that the New Testament writers rarely use the word *anēr* (man) when speaking about the incarnation; *anthrōpos* (human being) is much more common.[47] 'The important point about him is that he was the Word made Flesh, not the Word made Male.'[48]

Perhaps the crucial issue for women is not how to avoid the reality that Jesus came to earth as a man, but the implications of this fact. Does Jesus' maleness imply that women are inferior, or excluded from his ministry? We shall examine these themes in detail in chapter 7. For the moment, we may simply note that according to the gospels the good news is for women as well as men. The calling to be a follower of Jesus is not sex-specific.

The Spirit

In religious art, the third person of the Trinity is often depicted in female form. Elizabeth Cady Stanton's reformulation of the Trinity replaced the Spirit with Mother.[49]

More recently, the Woman's Creed, composed by Rachel Wahlberg, confesses belief in the 'Holy Spirit, the female Spirit of God'.[50] In many ways this is understandable, because the Spirit is the most elusive member of the Trinity, and is never described anthropomorphically. The Spirit is symbolized by breath, oil, water, wind, fire, a downpayment, a dove and a seal. These are all non-personal, genderless images.[51]

Rachel Wahlberg bases her confession on the fact that in Hebrew the word for 'spirit' is female. Genesis 1:2, 'the Spirit of God was hovering over the waters', becomes particularly significant because the word 'hovering' is used of the eagle 'that stirs up its nest and hovers over its young' (Dt. 32:11). It is assumed, therefore, that the first image of the Spirit in the Bible is a maternal one. This may be true, but we have to be careful to avoid the implication that the sexuality of the Godhead can be deduced from the gender of words. The gender of the Hebrew noun for 'spirit' in the Old Testament does not make the Spirit literally female any more than the gender of the Greek neuter noun for 'spirit' in the New Testament makes the Spirit impersonal.[52] In fact Jesus, as recorded by John, breaks the rules of Greek grammar to refer to the Spirit as 'he', thus emphasizing the personhood of the Spirit.

The bride and the bridegroom

A woman protested to me recently, 'God must be male because the Bible talks about Jesus as the bridegroom and the church as the bride.' Is this true?

Of course, the Bible is full of conjugal imagery. The Old Testament often portrays the link between God and his people as a marriage bond. Israel is the bride or wife and God is the husband.[53] In the New Testament, the church takes over Israel's role and is depicted as the bride of Christ.[54]

The Bible interprets the bride/bridegroom image for us.

It highlights God's compassion for his people (Is. 54:5–7), his rejoicing over them (Is. 62:5), and his faithfulness in the face of Israel's faithlessness (Ho. 1–3). The comparison of Christ to a bridegroom explains the oneness of Christ and the church and his self-giving on her behalf.[55]

But the Bible does not allow us to interpret the bride/bridegroom image as implying that God is literally male in relation to female Israel. Properly understood, the conjugal imagery does not define the gender of God. The prophet Hosea makes this abundantly clear. He employed both husband/wife and father/child images to explain the nature of God's relationship to Israel, but included the statement, 'I am God, and not man – the Holy One among you' (Ho. 11:9). The purpose of the imagery is not to establish God's gender but to explain in human terms the relationship between God and his people.

We have seen that God defies gender-stereotyping because, as spirit, God is beyond sexual distinctions and limitations. Biblical analogies, images and ways of addressing God do not make God either male or female. They serve as aids to understanding our relationship with God. Biblical imagery conveys God's personhood rather than God's gender. God embraces and transcends both paternal and maternal forms of parenthood. Seen in this light, Jesus' command to pray to God as 'Abba', 'Daddy', 'Papa', is neither oppressive nor alienating to women. There is no exclusively male or female angle on God. We have to evaluate our mental images of God and measure their accuracy against God's self-revelation in the Bible.

The same process of evaluation must be undertaken with our images of many biblical characters. This is particularly true of Mary, the central female figure in Christian tradition. Over the centuries, layers of meaning have been added to the sparse biblical account of her life. It is to her story that we now turn.

Notes

1 A. Walker, *The Color Purple* (Women's Press, 1983), pp. 164–8.

2 *E.g.* D. Spender, *Man-Made Language* (Routledge and Kegan Paul, 1980).

3 *E.g. The Inclusive-Language Lectionary*, prepared by the Inclusive-Language Lectionary Committee appointed by the Division of Education and Ministry, National Council of the Churches of Christ in the USA (John Knox Press, 1983).

4 *The Inclusive-Language Lectionary*.

5 Spender, *Man-Made Language*, p. 167.

6 *E.g.* D. Soelle, 'The Emancipation that Never Happened', in C. B. Fischer, B. Brenneman and A. McG. Bunnet (eds.), *Women in a Strange Land: Search for a New Image* (Fortress Press, 1975), pp. 84–5: 'One must ask why people speak and think of God in terms of such aseity and omnipotence. In order to answer this question we may use the method developed by Ludwig Feuerbach. He holds that this God corresponds to a deep-seated fantasy of mankind. Men, too, wish to be self-sufficient, autonomous, dependent on no one. They too would like to be omnipotent rulers. Probably all of us, even women, have dreams of omnipotence, but these dreams find their verbal expression in the religion fabricated by men in the interest of men.'

7 For a longer discussion see W. Rietkerk, 'Is God a Projection?', in *What in the World is Real?* (Communication Institute, 1982), pp. 211–25.

8 For a summary of this position see J. A. Phillips, *Eve: The History of an Idea* (Harper and Row, 1984), pp. 3–16.

9 Dt. 12:2–3; Jdg. 2:12–15; 10:6–10; Je. 7:18–19; 44:24–29; Is. 27:7–11.

10 For a longer discussion see M. Hayter, *The New Eve in Christ* (SPCK, 1987), pp. 14–8.

11 Is. 27:7–11; 43:15; 44:6; 45:21.

12 *E.g.* Dt. 16:21; 1 Sa. 7:3.

13 *E.g.* 2 Ki. 23:7; Je. 2:20.

14 Hayter, *New Eve*, pp. 14–8.

15 E. Campbell, *Sometimes I Get Scared: Psalm 23 for Children* (Pickering and Inglis, 1981).

16 For a longer discussion see A. E. Lewis (ed.), *The Motherhood of God* (St Andrew Press, 1984), pp. 11–5, and T. Smail, 'God: Motherly Father?', *CWN Series*, June 1, 1984.

17 Smail, 'Motherly Father'.

18 Mt. 5:16, 45–48; 6:7–8, 25–32; Mk. 11:25; Lk. 15:11–32; Jn. 11:41.

19 J. Jeremias, *New Testament Theology*, vol. 1 (SCM Press, 1971), p. 67.

20 Dt. 1:31; Ps. 103:13; Je. 31:9; Mal. 3:17.

21 Augustine, *Confessions* IV, 1, trans. R. S. Pine-Coffin (Penguin, 1961), p. 71.

22 Quoted in Lewis, *Motherhood*, p. 51.

23 Lewis, *Motherhood*, p. 52.

24 Lewis, *Motherhood*, p. 50.

25 E. C. Stanton (ed.), *The Woman's Bible* (1895: Polygon, 1985), p. 14.

26 Recorded by D. Spender in *Women Of Ideas (and What Men have Done to Them)* (Ark, 1982), p. 341.

27 For a helpful summary of this position see Lewis, *Motherhood*.

28 Dt. 32:11; Ho. 13:8.

29 Ps. 131:2; Is. 42:14; 49:15; 66:13.

30 M. Hebblethwaite, *Motherhood and God* (Geoffrey Chapman, 1984), p. 38.

31 On the imagery used to describe God see M. J. Evans, *Woman in the Bible* (Paternoster, 1983), pp. 21–2.

32 J. Blocher, *'La mère et Marie, mère de Jésus'*, recorded sermon, Église Évangelique du Tabernacle, Paris.

33 This argument is suggested by *The Inclusive-Language Lectionary*, appendix, p. 1.

34 S. T. Foh, *Women and the Word of God* (Presbyterian and Reformed Publishing Co., 1979), pp. 150–4. Foh develops this argument at length. She writes: 'The difference in comparison between paternal and maternal imagery is the difference between saying "God is our Father" (describing the person of God) and "God comforts his people as a mother comforts her child" (describing an action of God). In the former, God is identified ("is") by a noun "our Father". In the latter, an action of God is compared to ("as") an action performed by mothers.'

35 V. R. Mollenkott, 'Unlimiting God', *The Other Side*, 146, November 1983, p. 12.

36 Hayter, *New Eve*, p. 40.

37 *E.g.* C. J. M. Halkes, 'Biblical Authority in Feminist Perspective', WCC Amsterdam Consultation, December 1980; R. R. Ruether, *Sexism and God-talk* (SCM Press, 1983); L. M. Russell, *Feminist Interpretation of the Bible* (Basil Blackwell, 1985); E. S. Fiorenza, *In Memory of Her: A Feminist Theological Reconstruction of Christian Origins* (SCM Press, 1983).

38 Ruether, *Sexism and God-talk*, p. 85.

39 J. Tweedie, *In the Name of Love* (Granada, 1980), p. 123.

40 For a helpful discussion see Jeremias, *New Testament Theology*, vol. 1, p. 68.

41 For a longer discussion see E. M. Howe, *Women and Church Leadership* (Zondervan, 1982), pp. 83–4.

42 *E.g.* M. Daly, *Beyond God the Father* (Beacon Press, 1973), pp. 69–70.

43 V. R. Mollenkott, *Women, Men and the Bible* (Abingdon, 1977), pp. 62–3. She quotes 1 Corinthians 1:24, 30 which refer to Jesus as the 'wisdom of God' and 'wisdom from God', and links this with the personification of Wisdom in Proverbs 8.

44 For a fuller discussion see Foh, *Women and the Word*, pp. 155–8.

45 *E.g.* Is. 11:2; Lk 2:40; 1 Cor. 1:30; Col. 2:3; Rev. 5:12.

46 Mt. 11:19; Lk 7:35.

47 Mollenkott, *Women, Men and the Bible*, p. 61. L. Scanzoni and N. Hardesty, *All We're Meant to Be* (Word Books, 1973), p. 56.

48 E. Storkey, in Keay (ed.), *Men, Women and God*, p. 19.

49 Stanton, *The Woman's Bible*, Part I, p. 14.

50 Quoted in C. Marquet, *Femme et homme il les créa* (Les Bergers et les Mages, 1984), pp. 177–9.

51 For a fuller treatment see Foh, *Women and the Word*, pp. 160–3.

52 Foh, *Women and the Word*, pp. 160–3.

53 *E.g.* Is. 49:18; 54:5; 62:4; Je. 2:2; 3:20; Ezk. 16:8; Ho. 2:19–20.

54 2 Cor. 11:2; Eph. 5:23–33; Rev. 21:9; 22:17.

55 Eph. 5:22–32.

CHAPTER THREE

Mary –
ambivalent ideal

Merely a woman, yet
Whose presence, power is
Great as no goddess's
Was deemed, dreamed . . .[1]

MARY is the most prominent female figure in
Christianity. Her influence permeates every
aspect of Catholic cultures. 'Wayside shrines in
Italy . . . ; the Angelus bell in France; even the dedications
of village churches in England . . . are fragments of the
same myth that inspired Botticelli to paint the Virgin's
portrait, that raised the spire and towers of Chartres, and
that moved Dante to give voice in Paradise.'[2] But to what
extent does Mary provide a model for other women?

A few years ago I went in search of Mary in the Uffizi
Gallery in Florence. I was overwhelmed by different images
of the mother of Jesus. Room after room was hung with
paintings of annunciations, assumptions and heavenly cor-
onations. I discovered not one Mary but many Marys. The
paintings in the Uffizi reflect some of the traditions woven
around Mary. Her history has been shaped by different
emphases in theology and devotion. The story is an
intriguing one.

Virgin Mother

> Who can put Mary's high honour into words? She
> is both mother and virgin.[3]

In a church which was dominated by ascetism in the first
centuries, Mary epitomized the virtues of the celibate life.
As chaste virgin she provided the ideal to which all Christians should aspire. 'Let us love chastity above all things,'
Augustine wrote, 'for it was to show that this was pleasing
to him that Christ chose the modesty of a virgin womb.'[4]
Ambrose, Athanasius, Cyprian, Jerome, and Tertullian all
urged that Mary was to be imitated as a model of Christian
virginity. As early as 383 Jerome wrote a tract in which he
argued that Jesus was Mary's only child; he proposed that
the references to Jesus' brothers and sisters in the gospels
meant his cousins. In 451 Mary was declared ever virgin;
in 649 her perpetual virginity was declared a dogma of the
church. The dogma asserted Mary's virginity before,
during and after the birth of Christ. Mary was thus spared
the apparent defilement of sexuality. John Chrysostom,
commenting on the ever-virgin Mary, asked, 'What is
holier than she? Neither Prophets nor Apostles . . . neither
seraphim nor cherubim . . . nor any being visible or invisible.'[5] Mary was revered for her purity, holiness and ulti-
mate perfection.

The early Church Fathers honoured Mary as the New
Eve. Justin, Irenaeus and Tertullian in the second century
were the first to articulate this idea. Irenaeus of Lyons
(d. *c.* 202) wrote, 'Eve by her disobedience brought death
upon herself and on all the human race; Mary by her
obedience brought salvation.'[6] Death came through Eve,
life through Mary. For the Church Fathers, who interpreted the first sin as sexual, Mary's virginity repaired the
damage caused by Eve's sinful unchastity. Eve's sin, fallen
sexuality and death were contrasted with Mary's faith,
spotless virginity and life. Whereas Eve 'conceived the

word of the serpent',[7] Mary responded to the angel Gabriel, 'May it be to me as you have said.' Theologians used to point out that the angel's greeting 'Ave!' ('Hail!'), was the Latin name Eva reversed.

> That angel who greets you with 'Ave'
> Reverses sinful Eva's name.
> Lead us back, O holy Virgin,
> Whence the falling sinner came.[8]

From early centuries Mary was venerated not only as virgin but as the holy virgin mother of the Saviour. After fierce doctrinal disagreements at the Councils of Ephesus (431) and Chalcedon (451) about the nature of Christ as fully God and fully man, Mary was officially recognized by the title Mother of God (*Theotokos*, the God-bearer). The intention of both Councils was to clarify that Jesus was both God and man. From this time devotion to Mary grew as she was reverently admired for her holiness as Mother of God.

At the same time her cult absorbed many pagan strands as Mary took over the role of the ancient Mediterranean mother goddesses. Sites dedicated to the earth goddesses were rededicated to Mary.[9] Images, titles and rituals which formerly belonged to the goddesses were passed on to her. In the iconography of Mary, for example, the nursing madonna which appeared at an early date in Egypt is an adaptation of Isis nursing Horus.[10] Mary inherited the ancient titles of the goddesses as she became Queen of Heaven and Mother of God.[11] She took over the rites of fertility worship. As early as the third century Epiphanius mentioned an obscure sect, the Collyridians, who, like the worshippers of the Queen of Heaven (Je. 7:18), offered cakes to Mary.[12] Mary assumed the role of fertility goddess who must be invoked to assure fruitfulness and ease in childbirth. This is a continuing tradition. Our Lady of Montserrat near Barcelona is one of numerous madonnas celebrated for her reputed powers over fertility.

Queen of Heaven

> Virgin of virgins, I choose you today as my sove-
> reign, my queen, my empress.[13]

The Middle Ages were characterized by an emphasis on
Mary's role as Queen of Heaven, spiritual mother and
powerful intercessor. The gospels do not record Mary's
death; the medieval tradition of her escape from death and
bodily assumption into heaven was based on apocryphal
stories that circulated from the third century onwards. John
of Damascus in the eighth century explained; 'There was
a need that the body of her who in childbirth had preserved
her virginity intact, be preserved incorrupt after death.'[14]
The dogmas of Mary's perpetual virginity and assumption
hang together and sustain each other.[15] Once the assumption was accepted, Mary became a supernatural figure.
As ever virgin, triumphantly assumed body and soul into
heaven, Mary received the title Queen of Heaven. The
proof-text for the assumption is the ambiguous reference
in Revelation 12:1, 'A great and wondrous sign appeared
in heaven: a woman clothed with the sun, with the moon
under her feet and a crown of twelve stars on her head.'
Sometimes in art Mary is portrayed wearing a crown of
twelve stars and standing on the crescent moon. Numerous
paintings depict her heavenly coronation. She is crowned
by her Son or by the Trinity. Enthroned in heaven, Mary
became a type of the church triumphant. Her assumption
prefigured the assumption of the church.

Velázquez (1599–1660), *Coronation of the Virgin*, Prado,
Madrid. Mary assumes a regal role as she is crowned Queen
of Heaven. She has become a majestic figure far beyond
the reach of other women. In Velázquez's painting, the three
members of the Trinity participate in her coronation; Father
and Son together place the crown on her head while the Spirit
(represented as a dove) hovers over her.

As Queen of Heaven, Mary is a powerful intercessor on behalf of her earthly children. She stands between them and the judgment of God. Anselm described the Catholic view of Mary's mediatorial role perfectly: 'So the accused flees from the just God to the good mother of the merciful God.'[16]

Mary has the ear of Christ; he cannot refuse her. She is sure to obtain his favour. As spiritual mother of the church she sympathizes with her adopted children and pleads for them. She is an understanding, compassionate mother. Family relationships in a patriarchal Catholic family have been subtly projected on to the Godhead. Relationships in heaven mirror those below, where the powerful mother manipulates and controls her family. Barocci's painting, the *Madonna of the People*, graphically illustrates this. It portrays Mary suspended midway between heaven and earth. Beneath her a thronging crowd of men and women reach up to her imploringly. Above her, Christ sits in glory. Her hands stretched out to the people, Mary intercedes on their behalf. Christ in response raises his hand in blessing. Mary's intervention ensures forgiveness and assistance. Her appeals are always efficacious. The contrast with Eve is complete; Eve is the 'devil's gateway' but Mary is the 'portal of eternal mercy, the gate of heaven'.[17]

So personal devotion to Mary grew. Bernard of Clairvaux (d. 1153) was one of Mary's most ardent devotees. He confessed, 'There is nothing that delights me more than to speak on the glory of the Virgin Mother.'[18] As his Cistercian order spread across Europe, his intense, mystical love for Mary inspired a greater attachment to her. Bernard urged believers as slaves of Mary to follow their mistress:

Barocci (1528–1612), *Madonna of the People*, Uffizi, Florence. Mary becomes a powerful intercessor between God and the people. She is the gateway to heaven. At her request the Spirit descends.

Our queen has gone before us, and so glorious has been her entry into paradise that we her slaves, confidently follow our mistress, crying: Draw us after you and we shall run in the fragrance of your perfumes. As mother of our judge and mother of mercy, she will humbly and efficaciously handle the affairs of our salvation.[19]

In the age of chivalry, Marian devotion absorbed the ideals of courtly love celebrated by troubadour poetry. Mary assumed another identity as she became the beautiful lady of the heavenly court. She was addressed intimately as Our Lady.

Under the influence of the Franciscans in the thirteenth and fourteenth centuries Mary came to represent another ideal, that of poverty and humility. She shed the trappings of her royal status in heaven and became the Madonna of Humility. Mary was once more a simple peasant girl who was humbly obedient to God. Paintings of the Madonna of Humility show her kneeling barefoot before her infant Son or sitting on the ground. The backdrop of heavenly splendour has been replaced by a modest domestic scene.

The Protestant Reformers in the fifteenth century rejected invocation of Mary as Queen of Heaven and spiritual mother, but they too favoured this humble aspect of Mary. The Reformers restricted themselves to the imitation of Mary's obedience in the gospels and emphasized Mary's lowliness. Luther (d. 1546) wrote:

How should a creature deserve to become the Mother of God? Though certain scribblers make much ado about her worthiness for such motherhood, I prefer to believe her rather than them. She says her low estate was regarded by God, not thereby rewarding her for anything she had done, but, 'he has done great things for me'.[20]

Charonton and Villate (fifteenth century), *Virgin of Mercy*, Musée Condé, Chantilly. As all-powerful protectoress and merciful mother, Mary shelters believers under her cloak and answers their prayers. (Giraudon)

Protectress, co-redemptrix

> She is the great Pieta who casts her mother's cloak of mercy over our suffering humanity.[21]

As the cult of Mary reached its zenith in the Middle Ages, she evolved into an all-powerful protectress. She was portrayed as the Mother of Mercy sheltering her suffering children under her protective cloak. In paintings of the Mother of Succour, closely connected with the Mother of Mercy, the virgin protectress carries a club and battles with a devil who is trying to frighten a child. In paintings of both the Mother of Mercy and Mother of Succour, Mary appears as a huge, monumental figure who completely overshadows the mortals whom she is defending. Christ is absent from these pictures. Mary stands alone and invincible. She has become a refuge for sinners.

In the late Middle Ages Mary came to be honoured as

Mother of Sorrows. According to the gospel writers Mary
did not participate in Christ's passion, and only John records that she was present at the crucifixion. But John's
brief mention was developed in the stories of the stations
of the cross to give the impression that Mary was actively
involved in Christ's sacrifice. Mary's sufferings were par-
alleled to Christ's. She participated in and identified with
his passion. His passion became her passion. She was 'in-
separably joined to the saving work of her Son'.[22] Artists
painted her sharing Christ's sufferings in the stations of
the cross or receiving his broken body. As the cult of the
sorrows spread in the seventeenth century, Mary's sorrows
were officially set at seven. In the art of the period she

appears surrounded by these seven sorrows. Mary, Mother of Sorrows, collaborated so intimately with Christ in redemption that she became co-redemptrix. Benedict XV's apostolic letter (1918) is the classic statement on Mary's co-redemptive role: 'To such an extent did Mary suffer and almost die with her suffering and dying Son . . . that we may rightly say that she redeemed the human race together with Christ.'[23]

From the time of Augustine in the fourth to fifth centuries it was assumed that Mary was given an abundance of grace to conquer sin. Over the centuries this developed into the belief that Mary was free from original sin or immaculately conceived. According to Catholic teaching, Mary was perfectly sinless; she was incapable of sin. From the eighth century onwards, writers began to speak of Mary's immaculate conception. Andrew of Crete (d. 740) and John of Damascus (d. 749) are early examples. John of Damascus addressed Mary in these terms:

> O all-holy daughter of Joachim and Anne, you eluded the gaze of the principalities and powers and the flaming arrows of the Evil One. You dwelt in the bridal chamber of the Spirit and were kept unsullied that you might become the Bride of God and natural Mother of God. All-holy daughter, you made your appearance in your mother's arms, and you strike terror into the rebellious powers.[24]

He went on to develop the contrast between Eve and Mary, arguing that Mary was able to conquer Satan because she was free from sin. He said that Mary 'became the servant of God's will. She deceived the deceitful serpent and brought immortality into the world.'[25] This argument

Isenbrand, *Virgin of Seven Sorrows* (1551), Musées Royaux des Beaux-Arts de Belgique, Brussels. Surrounded by her seven sorrows, Mary is depicted as intimately sharing in Christ's suffering.

Tiepolo (1696–1770), *Immaculate Conception*, Prado, Madrid. Mary's head is crowned with twelve stars, and the crescent moon is under her feet. She appears invincible as she crushes the serpent underfoot.

is often repeated in the debate about the immaculate conception. Paintings of the immaculate conception sometimes depict Mary crushing the serpent under foot. Centuries of theological thought were dominated by controversy over the immaculate conception, which was eventually declared dogma in 1854.

By proclaiming Mary's perfect sinlessness, the dogma sets her apart from other human beings. The implications are that in Catholic tradition Mary became unique in her proximity to God. From her birth she was distinct. Her origin was quite different from that of the creatures over whom she exercises dominion. She was filled with grace from the first moment of her existence. Hers was a supernatural holiness.

The façade of Notre-Dame Cathedral in Paris, with its three doorways, provides a synthesis of the ways Mary has been perceived in the history of her cult. Above St Anne's doorway, seated on the throne of wisdom, she is a type of the church and as virgin mother presents her son to us. Over the north doorway the reliefs show Mary's assumption and coronation as Queen of Heaven. She is a token of hope to the church, as first of the saints to conquer death and gain eternal life. From heaven she acts as protectress for suffering humanity. Above the central doorway, Christ sits in judgment, while on his left Mary and John pray at the foot of the cross. Mary intercedes as spiritual mother.

Contemporary Marys

The spiritual motherhood of Mary is one of the dominant themes in the history of Mariology. Contemporary Catholicism has taken up this theme again. Pius X at the beginning of the century wrote on her spiritual motherhood, 'Mary is our sure way to Christ.'[26] The encyclical *Redemptoris Mater* (*Mother of the Redeemer*), which was written for the Marian year 1987–8, defines Mary's role. The encyclical emphasizes that Mary's position is subordinate to Jesus, but also insists on her maternal mediation. John Paul II has always cultivated devotion to Mary. He has reaffirmed her enormous significance in the history of the church: 'As a great sign that appeared in the heavens, in the fullness of time this woman dominates all history as the Virgin Mother of the Son and as Spouse of the Holy Spirit, as the Handmaid of humanity.'[27]

Pope John Paul is correct in noting that throughout the Catholic world Mary's influence has been all-pervasive. She has been the object of extravagant veneration and has inspired some of the finest artistic achievements in the Western world. Catholicism, by emphasizing Mary's unique supernatural role, has made her divine. In Catholic tradition, Mary is beyond the reach of ordinary women. By contrast, Protestants emphasize that according to the gospel accounts she is merely a woman. While Catholics may deify her, Protestants may unwittingly denigrate her. Although lip-service is paid to Mary as 'highly favoured', she may be practically ignored in Protestant churches. This is partly a reaction to the profound devotion of Catholics to her. Similarly, in the face of Protestant criticism, many Catholics become more entrenched in their attachment to Mary.

Catholics and Protestants may have become polarized in their views of Mary, but both traditions hold her up as a model of female submissiveness. She has become symbolic of the female virtues of passivity and renunciation. Women are encouraged to emulate her unobtrusive behaviour and reticence. Catholics and Protestants are agreed that Mary's humility and self-effacement are the ideal. Women, like her, should be retiring and silent.

Contemporary women are ambivalent in their attitudes to Mary. Many have reacted angrily to the traditional image of the mother of Jesus. Simone de Beauvoir protests at its damaging consequences for women: 'For the first time in human history, the mother kneels before her son; she freely accepts her inferiority. This is the supreme masculine victory consummated in the cult of the Virgin.'[28]

But the image of Mary kneeling before her son owes more to religious art than it does to the Bible. There is in fact no New Testament reference to Mary kneeling before Jesus, but there are several references to both men and women kneeling before him, when they recognize that he is God. Simone de Beauvoir sees the cult of Mary as essentially negative because, through it, women are subjected and beaten down. Women become passive and servile. This is especially true, argues Marina Warner, in fervently religious Catholic countries, where 'the more the menfolk swagger and command, the more the women submit and withdraw and are praised for their Christian goodness. Machismo, ironically enough, is the virgin's other face.'[29]

Not only is Mary a negative ideal. As far as women are concerned, she also represents an impossible ideal. Mary is idealized as the perfect woman. But how can ordinary women follow her example? Other women cannot be virgin mothers. 'Her freedom from sex, painful delivery, age, death and all sin exalted her above ordinary women and showed them up as inferior.'[30] As Queen of Heaven Mary is elevated far above the ranks of human women. Her sublime perfection highlights the imperfections of mortal women. She represents an unachievable ideal.

While recognizing that Mary has primarily been used as a negative symbol against women, Rosemary Radford Ruether, feminist theologian, selectively reinterprets the Marian cult to make Mary into a liberating symbol. 'If humanity male and female is to be redeemed, the female too must play a cooperating role in the work of salvation.'[31]

This emphasis on Mary as co-redemptrix may be taken a step further, so that Mary becomes the redemptive symbol for women. Just as male theologians have interpreted Mary to correspond with the traditional ideal, the archetype of the feminine, some feminists are reworking the ideal to fit their own ideological framework. Matriarchal characteristics are projected on to Mary; she becomes symbolic of female self-sufficiency and autonomy as she bears a child without male assistance.[32] Once again she is a mother goddess. The real historical woman is rejected in favour of deified femaleness.

Another feminist approach is to insist that Mary's story is a story about sisterhood. This approach concentrates on the real woman, our sister, rather than the idealized woman of Catholic tradition. Just as succeeding generations of Christians in different historical contexts have created images of Mary which reflect their own age, today she has become our sister. Providing it is not used for ideological ends, the sisterly approach to Mary is a positive one because it focuses attention on the historical woman.

Mary in the gospels

It requires a herculean effort of will to read Luke's infancy Gospel and blot from the imagination all the paintings and sculptures, carols and hymns and stories that add to Luke's spare meditation the hay and the snow and the smell of the animals' warm bodies as the Christ child was born that first Christmas night. Yet none of this circumstantial detail – with the exception of the swaddling bands – is present in the text. It is all the collective inheritance of western fantasy.[33]

It is difficult to discover the historical Mary among the plethora of pious images; the statues, shrines, icons, paintings and Christmas cards all clutter our imaginations. The historical facts about the real Mary who lived in the first century are scarce. There is little information about the details of her life. Her background and parentage are obscure. Her date of birth and the manner of her death are unknown. As we have seen, where the gospel accounts are silent, generations of scholars and speculators have been happy to fill in the gaps with theories and fanciful tales.

Mary makes few appearances in the gospels. She is most

visible in the accounts of Matthew and Luke, and appears only once in Mark and twice in John. Interestingly, Luke asserts: 'I myself have carefully investigated everything from the beginning' (Lk. 1:3). He may have questioned Mary about her life, for he describes some of her reactions to events. He tells us, for example, that she was 'greatly troubled' at Gabriel's words (Lk. 1:29), and that after hearing the angel's news that her relative Elizabeth had miraculously conceived and was six months pregnant, she quite naturally hurried off to visit her (Lk. 1:39). As events unfolded, Luke records that Mary treasured up all these things and pondered them in her heart (Lk. 2:19, 51).

From the gospels we know that Mary was a Galilean Jewess. Her name was Mary or Mariam. At the time of the annunciation she was betrothed to Joseph, a descendant of David.[34] According to Luke's detailed account, the angel Gabriel was sent to her in Nazareth with the news that she would become pregnant and give birth to a son (Lk. 1:26–38). Matthew tells us that Joseph was informed of the same news in a dream (Mt. 1:20–25). After Mary's visit to her cousin Elizabeth in the hill country of Judea (Lk. 1:39–56) and the birth of Christ in Bethlehem[35] she is mentioned on only a few occasions: at the purification in the temple, at the discovery of Jesus with the teachers of the law in the temple, at the wedding in Cana and at the cross.[36] Sometimes she is with Jesus' brothers.[37] She is referred to only once in the New Testament account of the early church, where she is named along with the disciples, the other women and Jesus' brothers who gathered in prayer after the ascension (Acts 1:14).

'The sum total of the Virgin's appearances in the New Testament is startlingly small plunder on which to build the great riches of Mariology.'[38] We have already noted that over the centuries the Catholic church has defined four dogmas about the Virgin Mary. She was declared Mother of God (451) and perpetually a virgin (649) by the early church Councils. Later her immaculate conception (1854) and assumption, body and soul, into heaven (1950) also became dogma. But only the dogma which proclaims her Mother of God is unequivocally derived from the New Testament. Since neither Mary's birth nor her death is described in the gospels, the dogmas of the immaculate conception and assumption can be supported only by inference. The first and the third gospels record that Mary was a virgin when Jesus was conceived but they do not confirm her perpetual virginity. The dogma of Mary's perpetual virginity relies heavily on the apocryphal *Book of James* which was in circulation by the second century. It was excluded from the New Testament canon because it was regarded as a forgery. According to the New Testament, Mary was never addressed by any of the titles that are employed in her cult, nor was she given a privileged position in the early church.

All four gospels record that Mary was the mother of Jesus. As mother of the Son of God, Luke's narrative records that the angel Gabriel greeted her as 'highly favoured' or 'full of grace' (Lk. 1:28). From the angel's greeting Catholic thinkers have built up a picture of Mary which emphasizes that she was conceived without sin and filled with grace from her birth. According to Catholic doctrine, since Mary was elected to be Mother of God, she was 'preserved from the inheritance of original sin'.[39] The New Testament never suggests that Mary was free from sin. Luke records that 'Mary was greatly troubled at his [the angel's] words and wondered what kind of greeting this might be' (Lk. 1:29). If Mary was singled out and sinless from birth she appears to have been unaware of it, unlike Jesus who from an early age knew that he had to be in his Father's house (Lk. 2:49).

When Mary and Elizabeth met, Elizabeth prophetically greeted Mary as 'blessed . . . among women' and 'the mother of my Lord' (Lk. 1:42–43). Mary responded with an intense song of praise to God (Lk. 1:46–55). Her song is reminiscent of Hannah's prayer (1 Sa. 2:1–10) and of some of the psalms which she would have heard in the synagogue from her childhood.

In her *Magnificat*, Mary revealed her own reactions to her pregnancy. She recognized the uniqueness of her role, saying, 'All generations will call me blessed.' Interestingly, she did not mention that she was about to become the mother of the Son of God. Rather, she concentrated on God. She rejoiced in God her Saviour and seemed to understand that her child would fulfil the promise to Abraham. Mary praised God as 'my Saviour, for he has been mindful of the humble estate of his servant. From now on all generations will call me blessed, for the Mighty One has done great things for me' (Lk. 1:47–49). She saw herself as the object of divine favour. By addressing God as her Saviour, Mary showed she is on a par with other sinners in need of a Saviour. Significantly, when Mary presented Jesus in the temple forty days after his birth, she offered 'a pair of doves or two young pigeons as a sin offering'.[40] As she celebrated in her song the way God overthrows human power structures, Mary seemed to identify with the 'hungry', the remnant of Israel who have longed for the coming of the Messiah.

Both Matthew and Luke record that Mary was a virgin when Jesus was conceived and that she remained one until his birth. The virgin birth was the culmination of the other miraculous births in the Old Testament and fulfilled Isaiah's prophecy that 'the virgin [or young woman] will be with child and will give birth to a son' (Is. 7:14). The conception of God in the flesh was quite different from all other conceptions. The conception of Jesus was distinct because he was conceived by the agency of the Holy Spirit. Mary's child was sinless. He did not share the inherited sinfulness of other human beings.

According to the New Testament, Mary was a married woman who had a number of children. Several passages refer to Jesus' 'brothers and sisters'; four of his brothers, James, Joses, Judas and Simon, are mentioned by name.[41] Matthew reports that Joseph 'had no union with her until she gave birth to a son' (Mt. 1:25), which seems to imply that their marriage was later consummated. This picture of Mary as a wife and mother of several children was an embarrassment to celibate clergy who regarded celibacy as a higher state than marriage. The New Testament account was, therefore, revised to create the impression that Mary remained a virgin after the birth of Jesus. Mary was deprived of all her children apart from Jesus. The brothers and sisters were explained away as relatives or Joseph's children by a 'fictitious first marriage'.[42] Jesus became Mary's only child. The 'until' in Matthew 1:25 was dismissed as not being 'a term of chronological intent'.[43]

The New Testament portrait of Mary depicts a woman who often appears to be bewildered by the behaviour of Jesus. She bears little resemblance to the powerful mediatorial figure who intercedes between humanity and her Son in traditional Catholic teaching. Several incidents are recorded which shed light on the relationship between Mary and Jesus. Luke recalls that when Jesus was twelve years old he went up to Jerusalem for the Passover with Mary and Joseph. Unknown to his parents, Jesus stayed behind in Jerusalem while they began their journey home. After a day's travelling they discovered that Jesus was not among the party of relatives and friends, and returned to Jerusalem to look for him. After three days of searching, 'they found him in the temple courts, sitting among the teachers, listening to them and asking them questions. Everyone who heard him was amazed at his understanding and his answers' (Lk. 2:46–47). Mary and Joseph were astonished. Mary asked him, 'Son, why have you treated us like this? Your father and I have been anxiously searching for you.' Jesus replied, 'Why were you searching for me? Didn't you know I had to be in my Father's house?' (Lk. 2:48–49). Mary and Joseph did not understand him. Were they confused by the reference to his divine Father or by his purpose on earth? We are not told. But Mary 'treasured all these things in her heart'.

From the beginning of his ministry, Jesus made it plain that he would not be controlled by his earthly family. Mark records that 'when his family heard about this, they went to take charge of him, for they said, "He is out of his mind" ' (Mk. 3:21). Jesus was not to be deterred. When he was told, 'Your mother and brothers are outside looking for you', he replied, 'Who are my mother and brothers?' 'Then he looked at those seated in a circle around him and said, "Here are my mother and my brothers! Whoever does God's will is my brother and sister and mother" ' (Mk. 3:31–35). In this confrontation Jesus gave preference to his spiritual family over his earthly family.[44]

On another occasion, 'a woman in the crowd called out, "Blessed is the mother who gave you birth and nursed you." ' Jesus' response puts Mary's maternal role in perspective. He replied, 'Blessed rather are those who hear the word of God and obey it' (Lk. 11:27–28). Jesus' answer, as in the family confrontation described in Mark, shifts our attention. He deflects the emphasis away from maternity to spiritual obedience. Mary is blessed not because of her functional, biological role but because of her obedience to the word of God.

The gospels record only one instance of Mary making a request to Jesus on behalf of others. When the wine had run out at a wedding in Cana of Galilee, Mary said to Jesus, 'They have no more wine' (Jn. 2:1–11). 'Dear woman, why do you involve me?' Jesus replied, 'My time has not yet come.' This conversation is similar to another, in which Jesus' brothers urged him to go to the Feast of Tabernacles and perform miracles. The brothers, unlike Mary, were sceptical and did not believe in him. Jesus replied to them, as he did to Mary, that his hour had not yet come (Jn. 7:2–9).[45] Jesus responded to both his mother's and his brothers' suggestions. But on both occasions he appears to have rejected family pressure to dictate the course of his ministry. After the miracle at Cana, Mary went with Jesus and his brothers to Capernaum, but she is not mentioned again until she reappears among the other women at the foot of the cross.

From the cross, Jesus addressed Mary, saying 'Dear woman, here is your son.' To John he said, 'Here is your mother.' John's Gospel records that 'From that time on, this disciple took her into his home' (Jn. 19:26–27). Mary was probably a widow by this time, so Jesus quite naturally entrusted her into the care of his closest disciple. From this dying wish of Jesus the Catholic church has developed the teaching that Mary is a spiritual mother to all believers. But there is no indication in the New Testament that the early church saw Mary in a maternal role. John understood Jesus to be speaking in a practical sense, and took Mary into his home.

In mariological teaching the events at Cana and Calvary take on enormous significance. Mary's role is interpreted symbolically rather than historically. At Cana she is interpreted as having actively intervened in the inauguration of Jesus' ministry by mediating as mother between people in need and her son. Traditional Catholic teaching holds that Mary is a figure of the future people of God, the future mother of the new Israel, the church. The water is taken to be the ritual water for purification which is changed into the wine, symbolic of the benefits brought through Christ.[46]

The Cana and Calvary narratives are read as being mutually explanatory. Jesus' words from the cross to Mary and John are taken as a declaration that the promise of Cana had come to fruition. The new covenant had replaced the old. John typifies the new people of God, Mary typifies the mothering church. These symbolic interpretations of Mary's role at Cana and Calvary are read into the historical narratives to create the image of Mary as a figure of the church and spiritual mother of believers. Luke's brief reference to Mary's presence in the upstairs room, praying with the disciples, women and Jesus' brothers after the ascension, has also been understood to mean that Jesus left her in a special role as mother to the early church (Acts 1:14). If this is the case, it is surprising that she disappears without further mention in the New Testament record of the early church.

In mariological teaching, the fact that Mary is addressed as 'woman' at the wedding in Cana and from the cross is thought to be significant. Mary is identified with the 'woman' spoken of in Genesis, whose offspring will crush the serpent's head, and with the vision of the pregnant 'woman' in Revelation.[47] This argument is developed to establish 'the unique place which she occupies in the whole economy of salvation'.[48] Mary's sorrow at the cross may fulfil Simeon's prophecy that 'a sword will pierce your own soul too' (Lk. 2:35), but there is no suggestion in the New Testament that while Jesus offered himself as a sacrifice for sins on the cross, Mary through faith offered her Son, thus co-operating in the work of redemption.

Mary, woman of faith

It is tragic that in all the theological controversy about Mary, we can lose sight of the Mary of Nazareth. Essentially she was a woman of faith whose faith cost her dearly. From the beginning of Luke's gospel her faith is obvious. Her believing acceptance of the angel's news contrasts with Zechariah's incredulity (Lk. 1:18–20, 34–38). In her prophetic greeting, Elizabeth blessed Mary for believing Gabriel's words, saying, 'Blessed is she who has believed that what the Lord has said to her will be accomplished!' (Lk. 1:45). Mary's own *Magnificat* demonstrates that she was faithfully waiting for the Messiah (Lk. 1:46–55).

Mary's faithful acceptance of God's purpose led her into painful and puzzling situations. From the moment she uttered the words, 'May it be to me as you have said' (Lk. 1:38), Mary's life changed dramatically. To begin with, there was the possibility of public disgrace and estrangement from Joseph (Mt. 1:18–19). Then, nine months pregnant, she had to travel from Nazareth to Bethlehem, only to discover that there was no room at the inn. She must have given birth in extreme discomfort and had to lay her newborn baby in a manger. Mary seems to have had difficulty making sense of the extraordinary events which were set in motion by the birth of her firstborn (Lk. 2:19).

On the night he was born, shepherds came to see him, saying they had seen a great company of the heavenly host who had told them about the child (Lk. 2:1–20). After the visit of the magi from the east Mary and Joseph were forced to flee into exile and live as refugees in Egypt (Mt. 2:1–18).

At Jesus' presentation in the temple Simeon prophesied to Mary: 'This child is destined to cause the falling and rising of many in Israel, and to be a sign that will be spoken against, so that the thoughts of many hearts will be revealed. And a sword will pierce your own soul too' (Lk. 2:34–35). These are terrifying words which Luke never fully explains. Was Simeon speaking of the deep anguish Mary will suffer as she watches what happens to her child?

At an early age Jesus caused his mother and father great anxiety when he disappeared in Jerusalem for three days, eventually to be rediscovered in the temple. Jesus' public ministry threw his family and local community into disarray. Mary may have witnessed the violent rejection Jesus suffered in his home village of Nazareth when, in reaction to his words in the synagogue, the people tried to throw him down the cliff (Lk. 4:14–30). She must have known too that some of Jesus' family thought that he was out of his mind and tried to take charge of him (Mk. 3:21).

For most of Jesus' ministry Mary was not present. We do not know what she made of the reports of Jesus' miracles and teaching that filtered back to her. But she was present as Jesus was tortured and taunted on the cross (Jn. 19:25–27). We cannot be certain if she saw her son after he had risen or if she learned of the resurrection at second hand. All we can be sure of is that Mary identified herself with the disciples, the women and Jesus' brothers waiting in prayer for the coming of the Holy Spirit (Act 1:14).

Mary's story is full of poignancy and pain. It is strange that she has been idealized in so many different ways. Mary of Nazareth is not sinless, or in some way removed from ordinary women. She is not Queen of Heaven, the token woman in the Trinity, or a goddess. She has no titles or special sway in heaven. She is neither a matriarchal nor a fertility symbol. She is just an ordinary woman who lived through something quite extraordinary. In fact it is Mary's ordinariness that makes her so extraordinary. We are to remember her as 'blessed among women'. As a woman of faith she is a powerful model for other women.

Mary may have been an ambivalent ideal for women, but Eve, the fallen woman, has been consistently used as a negative example. The sins of the mother are visited on the daughters; all women fall under the shadow of their foremother Eve. The facts about both Eve and Mary are few, but in both cases theologians have embellished their stories. The next two chapters unravel some of the threads in Eve's story.

Notes

1 Gerard Manley Hopkins, quoted in *New Catholic Encyclopedia*, vol. 9 (McGraw Hill Book Co., 1967), p. 385.

2 M. Warner, *Alone of All Her Sex* (Picador, 1976), pp. xxi–xxii.

3 Cyril of Alexandria, *Homily 4*, quoted in J. E. Rotelle, *Mary's Yes from Age to Age* (Collins, 1989), p. 57.

4 Quoted in Warner, *Alone of All Her Sex*, p. 54.

5 *New Catholic Encyclopedia*, vol. 9, p. 351.

6 Quoted in H. Bettenson, *The Early Christian Fathers* (Oxford University Press, 1956), p. 74.

7 Justin Martyr, quoted in J. A. Phillips, *Eve, The History of an Idea* (Harper and Row, 1984), p. 133.

8 Peter Damian (11th cent.), quoted in 'Eve and Mary: Conflicting Images of Medieval Woman', in N. Broude and M. D. Garrard (eds.), *Feminism and Art History* (Harper and Row, 1982), p. 84.

9 For a fuller discussion see R. R. Ruether (ed.), *Religion and Sexism* (Simon and Schuster, 1974), p. 179.

10 On the iconography of the Blessed Virgin Mary see *New Catholic Encyclopedia*, vol. 9, pp. 369–70.

11 Ruether (ed.), *Religion and Sexism*, p. 179.

12 On devotion to the Blessed Virgin Mary see *New Catholic Encyclopedia*, vol. 9, p. 364.

13 Bartolomé de los Ríos (d. 1652), quoted in Rotelle, *Mary's Yes*, p. 142.

14 Quoted in Warner, *Alone of All Her Sex*, p. 94.

15 The assumption was a firmly held Catholic belief for many centuries, but it was not declared a dogma of the church until 1950.

16 Quoted in Warner, *Alone of All Her Sex*, p. 315.

17 K. Rahner, quoted in Rotelle, *Mary's Yes*, p. 178.

18 Quoted in Warner, *Alone of All Her Sex*, p. 130.

19 St Bernard, *Homily 7 on Mary*, quoted in Rotelle, *Mary's Yes*, p. 90.

20 M. Luther, *Magnificat* 48–49, quoted in Rotelle, *Mary's Yes*, p. 131.

21 Edward Schillebeeckx, quoted in Rotelle, *Mary's Yes*, p. 186.

22 *De sacra liturgia* 103, quoted in *New Catholic Encyclopedia*, vol. 9, p. 364.

23 *New Catholic Encyclopedia*, vol. 9, p. 360.

24 Quoted in Rotelle, *Mary's Yes*, p. 76.

25 Rotelle, *Mary's Yes*, p. 76.

26 *New Catholic Encyclopedia*, vol. 9, p. 368.

27 Quoted in Rotelle, *Mary's Yes*, p. 187.

28 S. de Beauvoir, *The Second Sex* (1949: Penguin, 1972), p. 203.

29 Warner, *Alone of All Her Sex*, p. 183.

30 Warner, *Alone of All Her Sex*, p. 153.

31 R. R. Ruether, *Mary – The Feminine Face of the Church* (SCM Press, 1979), p. 54.

32 M. Daly, *Beyond God the Father* (Beacon Press, 1973), pp. 69–70.

33 Warner, *Alone of All Her Sex*, pp. 13–4.

34 Mt. 1:18; Lk. 1:27.

35 Mt. 1:18 – 2:12; Lk. 2:1–20.

36 Lk. 2:21–40, 41–52; Jn. 2:1–11; 19:26–27.

37 Mt. 12:46–50; Mk. 3:31–35; Lk. 8:21.

38 Warner, *Alone of All Her Sex*, pp. 13–4.

39 John Paul II, *Redemptoris Mater* (Catholic Truth Society, 1987), p. 21.

40 Lk. 2:22–24; *cf.* Lv. 12:8.

41 Mt. 12:46–48; Mk. 3:31–35; 6:3; Lk. 8:19–21; Jn. 7:1–5; 1 Cor. 9:5; Gal. 1:19.

42 On Mary's perpetual virginity see U. Ranke-Heinemann, *Eunuchs for Heaven: The Catholic Church and Sexuality*, trans. J. Brownjohn (André Deutsch, 1990), pp. 307ff.

43 For a fuller discussion see *New Catholic Encyclopedia*, vol. 9, p. 338.

44 On this interpretation see H. Blocher, 'Marie, Mère de Jésus dans le Nouveau Testament', *Tychique*, 56 (Communauté du Chemin Neuf, Lyon, 1985), p. 48.

45 Blocher, 'Mère de Jésus', p. 47.

46 *New Catholic Encyclopedia*, vol. 9, p. 344.

47 Gn. 3:15; Rev. 12:1–6.
48 John Paul II, *Redemptoris Mater*, pp. 50–1.

CHAPTER FOUR

Not in God's image, spare rib, and all that

The story of Eve is, in a sense, at the heart of the concept of Woman in Western civilization.[1]

THE Genesis account of Eve's creation and fall has been retold in countless ways. Her story has had a pervasive influence on Western culture.[2] But who was Eve? The question is not an easy one to answer. A confusing number of Eves emerge from the various interpretations of Genesis. It would be almost impossible to catalogue all the different guises in which she has appeared.

Feminist theologians argue that common to all the traditional interpretations is a misogynist bias. They are currently producing new interpretations as a reaction to the negative sexualization of Eve. The original language, symbols and imagery are being reworked from matriarchal, sociological, and psychoanalytical perspectives.[3]

It is hardly surprising that Eve has been perceived in so many different ways, since biblical interpretation is fraught with pitfalls. Interpretation easily becomes over-interpretation, as the theologian reads into the text personal misconceptions and prejudices to manipulate the facts and subtly weight the evidence. Nowhere is this tendency more marked than in the history of the interpretation of Genesis.

The first chapter contains a brief statement about the creation of man and woman in God's image and their purpose on earth (Gn. 1:26–28). Genesis 2:18–25 describes in greater detail the creation of woman and Genesis 3:1–24 is an account of the fall. These passages are crucial to the biblical understanding of woman, since they outline God's original intention in creating man and woman and the results of their alienation from God. But, from the same sequence of events, theologians have variously argued the case for woman's inferiority, for the equality of the sexes, and more rarely for woman's superiority. We will call the two standard versions, which argue for woman's inferiority or for her equality, the traditional and egalitarian interpretations.

The traditional interpretation

In the traditional interpretation, the statement in Genesis 1 about both man and woman being made in God's image and given shared responsibility for the earth is minimized or relativized in the light of Genesis 2. The second chapter is interpreted as teaching that woman is subordinate and even inferior. This is not stated explicitly in the text, but the following facts, which we shall examine in detail later, are taken as evidence of woman's secondary role.[4]

1. Adam was created before Eve.
2. Eve was made for Adam, to be his helper.
3. Eve was created from Adam.
4. Adam named her Woman.

This evidence is used to produce an ambivalent or negative view of Eve, who is less like God, more carnal and less spiritual than Adam. The implication is that the woman has an inherent imperfection. She is, therefore, more open to temptation and deception.

So the scene is set for Genesis 3, with Eve at centre stage. She is the obvious butt of Satan's wiles. The impression of Eve's inferiority is confirmed by emphasizing that she is the first to sin and seduces Adam to sin. Her sin is seen as more serious and her punishment more severe, whereas Adam is often presented as more sinned against than sinning. Paul's comments on Genesis 1 – 3 in the New Testament are taken as further proof of woman's inferiority.[5]

This interpretation tends to absolutize the differences between the sexes, making them appear all-important. Adam and Eve have little in common. Adam is far superior to his partner. Eve is a lower order of creation.

The egalitarian interpretation

Egalitarian interpreters see the equality of man and woman in Genesis 1 as emphasized and not depreciated by the second chapter. Genesis 2 is interpreted as a complementary and egalitarian account since it contains no explicit statement of Adam's superiority or Eve's subordination. Genesis 3 is seen as portraying man and woman as equally guilty. Paul's comments in the New Testament are interpreted so that they do not contradict this view. Galatians 3:28 is emphasized because it states that 'there is neither . . . male nor female, for you are all one in Christ Jesus'.[6]

At its most extreme, this interpretation tends to relativize the differences between the sexes, underlining the similarities between man and woman. Any distinctions between the sexes are minimized.

Not in God's image?

> Of Nature her th'inferiour, in the mind
> And inward Faculties, which most excell,
> In outward also her resembling less
> His Image who made both, and less expressing
> The character of that Dominion giv'n
> Ore other Creatures.[7]

A feminist history of women in Western societies argues that one of the most powerful forces shaping the way women have been viewed, and have viewed themselves, is the belief that woman is not, or is only partly, in God's image. Hence the title of the book *Not in God's Image*.[8] Sadly, some of the most prominent theologians in the past have been guilty of propagating this dogma. For example, in the fourth century Augustine pronounced:

> The woman together with her own husband is the image of God, so that the whole substance may be one image; but when she is referred separately to in her quality of help-meet, which regards the woman herself alone, then she is not the image of God; but as regards the man alone, he is the image of God as fully and completely as when the woman too is joined with him in one.[9]

This is consistent with Augustine's dualistic view of humanity. He argued that, just as the individual is divided into the mind and the concupiscence, the same is true of the two sexes. Man is the mind, ruler and lord; he is concerned with higher things. Woman is the concupiscence, to be ruled and subject; she is concerned with lower things. Taken out of man and separated from him, woman ceases to be in God's image.[10]

Aquinas too in medieval times argued:

> The image of God, in its principal signification, namely the intellectual nature, is found both in man and in woman. But in a secondary sense the image of God is found in man, and not in woman: for man is the beginning and end of woman; as God is the beginning and the end of every creature.[11]

Paradoxically, these formative thinkers insisted that the human race as a whole is in God's image but the female half of the race shares God's image in a different and secondary way. Man is the real human being, made fully in God's image. Woman's identity is defined in relationship to man, hers is a reflected glory. Woman is inferior and dependent. In other words, there is something wrong with woman. This medieval misogynism survived into the Reformation period. The Reformers expressed the same view in a modified form. They dismissed the more fanciful interpretations of Genesis, but they, too, insisted that woman was created inferior.

Calvin, writing about woman having been created as a help, came to the rather ambivalent conclusion that 'woman also, though in the second degree, was created in the image of God'.[12] He made the same point in his eleventh sermon on Job. 'Women', he said, 'are in the image of God in an inferior degree.'[13] In the same sermon he went on to explain that though God made both men and women in his image, 'men are preferred to females in the human race. We know that God constituted man as the head and gave him a dignity and preeminence above that of the woman . . . It is true that the image of God is imprinted on all; but still woman is inferior to man.'[14]

Calvin stated that both sexes are in the divine image, but he was careful to qualify this by saying that as an image-bearer the female is inferior to the male. Woman mirrors less of her creator. He assumed that male headship, which is spoken of by Paul in the New Testament, implies that females are from creation inferior. (We will deal with the meaning of headship in chapter 8 on Paul.) But Genesis, in contrast to Calvin, states that man and woman bear God's image in the same way.

Why were these men so intent on making woman appear less like God? They have been accused of deliberately falsifying the facts to give a misogynist reading to the text, their motivation being that 'there would have been little to gain as far as males were concerned by propagandizing the version which had God make human beings in God's image, female and male. Given this imagery of equality, Adam would have to share his place with Eve.'[15] This is too hard. But undoubtedly, male theologians have often allowed their thinking about women to be clouded by the male-dominated cultures in which they have lived. Beginning with the axiom that woman is inferior to man, they have found evidence for this in the text.

In the same way, theologians today may produce interpretations which are constructs of the late twentieth century, reflecting contemporary culture. In contrast with and in reaction to the traditional interpretations of Genesis 1, some theologians suggest that in the beginning there was an original androgynous or bisexual *adam* who fell into sexual dividedness. Thus the existence of male and female is the result of sin.[16]

The goal is then to recover the ideal androgyny; wholeness is achieved by becoming both male and female. This is a key concept in the women's movement because of its emphasis on humanity as sexually undifferentiated. Rosemary Radford Ruether explains, 'Women seek a reconstruction of relationships for which we have neither words nor models: a reconstruction which can give each person the fulness of their being stolen from them by false polarization. The term for this in the women's movement is androgyny.'[17]

The traditional interpretation tends to absolutize the difference between the sexes, making Adam far superior and Godlike. It insists that from her creation woman is inferior to man and mirrors less of her creator. From the beginning woman is subject to her superior, man. The interpretation which emphasizes an androgynous ideal, however, minimizes sexual differences by making *adam* bisexual.[18] Both interpretations find little support in Genesis 1.

> Then God said, 'Let us make man in our image, in our likeness, and let them rule over the fish of the sea and the birds of the air, over the livestock, over all the earth, and over all the creatures that move along the ground.'

79

So God created man
in his own image,
in the image of God
he created him;
male and female
he created them.

God blessed them and said to them, 'Be fruitful and increase in number; fill the earth and subdue it. Rule over the fish of the sea and the birds of the air and over every living creature that moves on the ground.' (Gn. 1:26–28)

This passage is clearly a declaration of equality. Man (*adam*) in the plural, generic sense is made male and female in God's image. Sometimes confusion arises because of the way Genesis 1:26–28 alternates between the singular, plural and collective. Genesis 5:1–2 helpfully expands on Genesis 1 and makes it obvious that male and female together were called *adam*. It reads: 'When God created man, he made him in the likeness of God. He created them male and female and blessed them. And when they were created, he called them "man" [*adam*].'

The Bible's first statement about man and woman not only makes it abundantly clear that both sexes are in the divine image, but that from the beginning there was sexual differentiation. *Adam* (mankind) was not one androgynous creature, but two creatures, male and female. Sexuality was not the result of the fall; it was there from the beginning.[19]

Man and woman equally and jointly reflect their creator. There is no hint of woman being a second-rate image-bearer or of man being more Godlike. They share a common humanity as they are made in the image of God. Woman is fully in God's image and fully human. She is defined primarily not in terms of her relationship to man, but in terms of her relationship to God, because, like man, she is made in God's image.

Man and woman, made in the image and likeness of

God,[20] share a unique position in the created order. They are like God, but we are never told exactly how they resemble their creator. Generations of theologians have wrangled over definitions of the image.[21] Essentially, all that makes man and woman distinctively human, such as their spiritual, moral, rational, creative characteristics, and their capacity to love and communicate, can be equated with the image of God. Both sexes together stand apart from the rest of creation in being uniquely like God.

Equal dominion

God gave two commands to the first couple in Genesis 1. He told them to be fruitful and to rule over the earth. These commands were given to both the man and the woman. There has been a persistent tendency, however, to apply the command to procreate to woman, but to exclude her from the command to exercise dominion or rule over the earth. John Chrysostom, writing in the fourth century, voiced this belief:

> Since our lives consist of two kinds of affairs, public and private, the Lord has divided the task between man and woman: to her he has assigned the responsibility of the home, while to the man is assigned the affairs of the state.[22]

Woman was dismissed from public life and relegated to the domestic sphere. This view has prevailed throughout church history. In the Reformation period, Calvin, perceiving that the commands in Genesis 1 are given 'to them', took the plural to refer to Adam's posterity, rather than concede that both man and woman are being addressed. In his commentary on Genesis he wrote, 'The use of the plural number intimates that this authority was not given to Adam only, but to all his posterity as well as to him.'[23] This interpretation is not very convincing. Calvin assumed that woman was not included in the command, so he devised a tortuous explanation for the plural that is in the text.

Luther made the same assumption about woman's role. In a letter written in August 1524 to three nuns whom he was encouraging to abandon the cloister, Luther set out a woman's purpose in life:

> God fashioned her body so that she should be with a man, to have and to rear children. The words of Genesis 1:26–28 plainly indicate this, and parts of her body show God's purpose . . . therefore let this suffice. No woman should be ashamed of that for which God made and intended her.[24]

In a sense, Luther's views were progressive because he did not exhort women to renounce marriage, and countered the church's elevation of celibacy as the Christian ideal. Instead of regarding marriage as a concession to the frailty of the flesh, Luther affirmed that marriage was ordained by God in creation. Yet at the same time, Luther limited women's roles. Elsewhere he expanded on this:

> Men have broad shoulders and narrow hips, and accordingly they possess intelligence. Women have narrow shoulders and broad hips. Women ought to stay at home; the way they were created indicates this, for they have broad hips and a wide fundament to sit upon, keep house and bear and raise children.[25]

Often women's lives have been limited and confined by decree of the church. Some have voiced deep regret that so many areas of life have been closed to them. The heroine of one nineteenth-century novel, realizing the extent to which she is restricted by her puritanical husband, complains bitterly, 'It is a great curse to have been born a woman.'[26] The questions and frustrations about women's roles are still with us. Almost always in seminars on the subject someone asks, 'Does the Bible teach that women must stay at home?' The Bible does teach that mothers and fathers are to love and care for their children. Yet, despite Luther's observations about the broad fundament of a German *Hausfrau*, there is nothing in Genesis 1 to suggest that women should be excluded from the mainstream of human activity and that their only occupations should be housework and childcare. Quite the opposite is true. Neither of the two commands about creation and dominion or ruling the earth is sex-specific.

Elizabeth Cady Stanton, writing at a time of great ferment about women's rights, put it beautifully:

> Equal dominion is given to woman over every living thing, but not one word is said giving man dominion over woman. Here is the first title deed to this green earth given alike to the sons and daughers of God.[27]

A mere afterthought?

Initially, Genesis 1 – 2 may appear to give contradictory accounts of creation. One of the apparent differences is that in Genesis 1 male and female seem to be created simultaneously, while in Genesis 2 woman is created after man. The traditional interpretation has stressed Genesis 2, whereas the egalitarian interpretation has stressed Genesis 1.

The two chapters contain differences of emphasis rather than contradictions. Genesis 1 gives a day-by-day account of creation, in which we are told that man and woman were created on the same day. Genesis 2 gives a more detailed account of events on the sixth day. Genesis 1 explains the relationship man and woman have with God, declaring that they are equally in God's image, with no suggestion of one sex being more like God. Genesis 2 focuses on the relationship that they have with each other:

it also fills out details of the creation of woman.

> The LORD God said, 'It is not good for the man to be alone. I will make a helper suitable for him.'
>
> Now the LORD God had formed out of the ground all the beasts of the field and all the birds of the air. He brought them to the man to see what he would name them; and whatever the man called each living creature, that was its name. So the man gave names to all the livestock, the birds of the air and all the beasts of the field.
>
> But for Adam no suitable helper was found. So the LORD God caused the man to fall into a deep sleep; and while he was sleeping, he took one of the man's ribs and closed up the place with flesh. Then the LORD God made a woman from the rib he had taken out of the man, and he brought her to the man.
>
> The man said,
>
> > 'This is now bone of my bones
> >   and flesh of my flesh;
> > she shall be called "woman",
> >   for she was taken out of man.'
>
> For this reason a man will leave his father and mother and be united to his wife, and they will become one flesh.
>
> The man and his wife were both naked, and they felt no shame. (Gn. 2:18–25)

Woman was created after man. Does this mean that she is of less significance and worth? Is she merely an afterthought? Some theologians make so much of Adam's privileges and self-sufficiency as the first-formed that woman, formed after him, appears very second rate.[28] Philo of Alexandria (c. AD 50) even suggested that woman's creation was a calamity:

Woman becomes for him the beginning of a blame-worthy life. For as long as he was by himself, as accorded with such solitude he went on growing like to the word and like God.[29]

Feminist theologians prefer to see woman as the pinnacle or crown of creation. From their perspective the six days reached their climax with the creation of woman; without her, creation was incomplete.[30] She was the culmination of creation. Since in the first chapter it is the one who was created last who was given precedence, it is argued that the same principle applies in chapter 2 and that creation moved to a climax with the creation of woman. The contributors to *The Woman's Bible* marshalled their arguments cleverly; they are often repeated by modern feminist theologians. They claimed that the order of creation was no argument for Adam's superiority, since if superiority were based on order of creation Adam would be subject to the animals and the earth.

Lillie Devreux Blake argued:

It cannot be maintained that woman was inferior to man even if, as asserted in Chapter 2, she was created after him without at once admitting that man is inferior to the creeping things, because created after them.[31]

Despite its apparent reasonableness, this is a weak argument, for the distinction between animals and men and women is very clear; men and women are to rule over the animals and the earth.

Phyllis Trible, in an intricate argument, reasons that man does not precede woman in creation since *adam*, the human being at the beginning of chapter 2, is sexually undifferentiated. *Adam* contains the potential for the creation of woman and is a kind of proto-humanity. So woman was in a real sense present from the beginning. Only after Genesis 2:22 is gender mentioned. Man is referred to as '*ish*, man as male in relation to the woman.[32]

In contrast, Stephen B. Clark uses the fact that *adam* means the human at the beginning of chapter 2 to focus on the importance of man as male:

> Genesis 2 is talking about a man who was the first human being and from whom the whole human race descended. At this point he was the human race. Later on, his proper name was 'human' or 'man' (Genesis 5:1–3). The writers of Scripture understood him as embodying in his person the human race, much as the man Israel embodied in his person the people Israel (*cf.* Hebrews 7:9).[33]

What he says is, in a sense, correct. But he goes on to insist that man, the first-formed, is the central character of the Genesis narrative. God treats him as a Jewish father would treat his son. He finds him a good job and a wife. There can be no doubt that the son occupies a specially privileged position. In all this Clark implies that Adam's relationship to God is closer than the relationship of his wife. Clark exaggerates Adam's position by emphasizing that he is the embodiment of the race, God's son and the central character in the story. This completely distorts Genesis 2.

Phyllis Trible plays down the order in creation and argues that male and female were created simultaneously, to relativize sexual differences. In contrast, Clark's interpretation over-emphasizes the order of creation so that Adam appears far superior to his wife. We cannot evade the fact that the order of creation exists, but it is also true that man and woman have the same origin. There are no grounds for a contemptuous attitude to woman.

How significant is it, then, that man preceded woman in the order of creation? Genesis does not answer this question. We will take up the subject again when we discuss Paul's use of Genesis 2.[34] But, to return to our original question, it is clear from Genesis that the woman was not a mere afterthought. The first sentence spoken by God in the account of the creation of woman is a surprising one. He declared, 'It is not good for the man to be alone.' This is the only negative note in the account of creation.[35] It stands in stark contrast to all the declarations that successive stages of creation were 'very good'. Someone was missing. A solitary man was not self-sufficient. The creation of woman was a necessity. Woman is indispensable; she is not an afterthought. From the beginning human beings were created for relationship.

A helper suitable for him

The Genesis 2 account records that God created woman as a 'helper suitable' for man. The word 'helper' or 'help' has been variously understood in the history of biblical exegesis. Writing in the third century, Clement said:

> Moreover, women must, with their own hands, bring from the pantry whatever we need. And it is not dishonourable for them to work at the millstone, nor to tend to the food preparation in order to be pleasing to their husbands; nor is the spouse to be disapproved of who keeps her house and is a help-meet to her husband.[36]

Woman was given to man as helper, he says, 'for the sake of begetting children and looking after domestic affairs'.[37]

Both Augustine and Aquinas placed similar limits on woman's activities and at the same time denigrate woman's spirituality. According to Aquinas, woman is a functional object for man's use.

> Woman was made to be a help to man. But she was not fitted to be a help to man except in generation, because another man would prove a more effective help in anything else.[38]

Calvin rejected the view that woman is a functional object given to man 'only for the companion of his chamber'; rather he insisted that woman is to be the 'inseparable associate of his life'.[39] But this does not make her man's equal, for according to Calvin woman is innately inferior to man.

> Woman was created later to be a kind of appendage to the man on the express condition that she should be ready to obey him, thus . . . God did not create two heads of equal standing but added to the man a lesser helpmeet.[40]

'Helpmeet' has, therefore, invariably been taken to mean an inferior or a help in the house. But the words that are used in Genesis do not imply domesticity, subservience or even inferiority. Woman is called *ezer*, usually translated 'help' or 'helper'. This translation is rather misleading, because 'helper' in English suggests an inferior assistant, whereas the Hebrew word *ezer* does not have this connotation. Fifteen of the twenty-one occurrences of *ezer* in the Old Testament refer to *God* as 'help'.[41] The Psalmist, for example, speaks of God as 'an ever-present help in trouble' (Ps. 46:1).[42] So the term if anything *favours* woman. She is described not only as *ezer*, but as *ezer kenegdo* which means 'a help fit for, corresponding to or adequate to'. She is man's counterpart, companion or partner, neither superior nor inferior to him. What is emphasized in the designation of woman as a help suitable for the man is the complementarity and reciprocity of their relationship. They are equal but different. Exactly how the woman is to complement the man is not specified. There is no stereotype.

Spare rib

Not only was woman made as a help *for* the man but she was made *from* him. Susan Brooks Thislethwaite tells the story of a woman who was severely abused by her husband for many years. When she complained of her injuries he replied, 'Your bones are my bones – just like it says in the Bible.'[43] This is a shocking misrepresentation of what Genesis actually says, but the traditional interpretations have certainly tended to portray woman as inferior, incidental and inessential. Since she is derived from man it is assumed that she is an extension of him and that he owns her. Woman becomes a very different, lower order of creation.

In the Jewish Midrash, for example, one of the rabbis says, 'The beginning of man's downfall is sleep', since it was during his sleep that woman was created.[44] Another rabbi explains that 'woman made from bone needs perfume since bones putrify. She also has a shrill voice because a bone dropped in a hot pot makes a crackling sound.'[45]

The Church Fathers, with their dualistic view of soul and body, man and woman, tended to use the woman as a symbol of the body in relation to the soul. For Augustine, Eve taken from Adam's side symbolizes the lower, corporeal side of man.[46] The differences between man and woman are overstated. In *The City of God* he gives an exaggerated, allegorical interpretation of Eve's creation. Adam's deep sleep is compared to the suffering of Christ on the cross. Adam suffers so that his bride may come into being.[47] This interpretation, which is typical of the Fathers, reinforced the idea that man is more Godlike and noble than woman.[48]

Not only has it been argued that because of the way she was created woman is intrinsically of less worth, but at a practical level commentators have used woman's derivation from the man to press her into a silent and submissive role. Matthew Henry, the eighteenth-century commentator, for example, wrote, 'She was made of the man, and for the man, all which are urged there as reasons for the humility, modesty, silence and submissiveness, of that sex in general.' Perhaps he was shocked at his own severity, for in the next breath he added, 'She is the crown, a crown to her husband, the crown of the visible creation. The man was dust refined, but the woman was dust double refined, one remove further from the earth.'[49]

Feminist theologians question the view that woman, since she was derived from man, is necessarily inferior to him. Elizabeth Cady Stanton challenged this would-be proof of woman's inferiority by asking, 'Grant it, then, as the historical fact is reversed in our day, and the man is now of the woman, shall his place be one of subjection?'[50] She appears to be making a point similar to that of the apostle Paul, who, when he referred to this event, said, 'In the Lord, however, woman is not independent of man, nor is man independent of woman. For as woman came from man, so also man is born of woman. But everything comes from God' (1 Cor. 11:11–12).

Paul's last sentence is very important. Ultimately, woman is not 'out of' (*ek*) man but 'out of' (*ek*) God. This is the fundamental truth about both sexes.[51] Both man and woman are created by God. The primary relationship is with God. Sexual differentiation can be understood only in the light of man's and woman's relationship with God. Without this understanding of man and woman there is a tendency either to negate sexual differentiation as unimportant or to regard it as all-important.

Significantly, the man in his deep sleep was completely passive and oblivious of the woman's creation. He had no control over her birth. Both sexes owe their creation entirely to God.[52]

We are never told why Eve was constructed from Adam's side. Christine de Pizan, one of the fourteenth century's most learned women, suggested:

There Adam slept, and God formed the body of the woman from one of his ribs, signifying that she should stand at his side as a companion and never lie at his feet like a slave, and also that he should love her as his own flesh.[53]

Woman was taken from Adam but this does not make her less than him any more than Adam's creation from the earth makes him less than the dust.[54] Man and woman are of the same essence. They are of the same kind. Calvin saw the significance of this. He pointed out that 'if the two sexes had proceeded from different sources, there would have been occasion either of mutual contempt or envy or contentions'.[55] Given their common origin there can be no grounds for either sex to feel superior.

A great deal has been made of woman being no more than a male rib. In fact, the Hebrew word, as well as meaning 'rib', can be translated 'flank' or 'side'. Other biblical writers never use the word 'rib'. For example, Paul simply says that woman is from man (1 Cor. 11:8). The author of Genesis seems to be playing with the double meaning of the word 'rib', which may mean 'side' and even 'alter ego'.[56]

Adam greeted Eve enthusiastically, even ecstatically. At last she was here. His greeting underlines their common humanity. In all the zoological parade, he had not found a companion. The animals are a separate order of creation. For the first time he was able to speak in the first person.[57] He recognized her as 'bone of my bones and flesh of my flesh'. Adam lapsed into poetry as he met his wife. She was a 'mirror of himself'.[58] Adam's greeting affirms their unity. He called her 'woman', 'isha, because she was taken out of man, 'ish. The play on words emphasizes their similarity. She was not a separate species; she was related to him in a way that the animals were not. Woman is not so much the opposite sex or the second sex as the neighbouring sex.[59] She is uniquely like man. The whole account stresses the interdependence and complementarity of man and woman rather than man's independence or woman's inferiority. This is a partnership in which both partners are equal but different. The pun of 'isha, 'woman', on 'ish, 'man', emphasizes their unity and diversity.

She shall be called woman

Adam named the animals; he also named his helper 'woman'. Later he gave the woman the personal name Eve. This has been interpreted as a demonstration of man's rule over woman.[60] Naming was an important function in the Old Testament. The prerogative of naming belonged to the one who was in a position of authority and to whom deference was due. On several occasions, for example, God exercised his lordship by naming or changing the names of his followers.[61] So, it is argued, Adam showed he was in a position of authority over the animals and woman by naming them. Woman was another creature over whom Adam was lord.

But is man's naming of woman parallel to his naming of the animals? Does the naming of the woman indicate man's headship, superiority or rule?

Phyllis Trible argues that the naming of woman and the naming of the animals are not comparable. She reasons that in the Old Testament, when the naming is authoritative, a standard formula is employed, made up of the verb 'to call' and the noun 'name'.[62] For example, Genesis 4:25 literally reads: 'She bore a son and called his name Seth.' In Genesis 2 the animals are named according to this standard formula. But Genesis 2:23 states simply, 'She shall be called woman.' There is no mention of the noun 'name'. In fact, woman was not given her personal name until Genesis 3:20, when, after the fall, Adam called his wife's name Eve according to the standard formula. Phyllis Trible concludes that in Genesis 2, 'in calling the woman, the man is not establishing power over her but rejoicing in their mutuality'.[63]

Is there a significant difference between the calling of woman in Genesis 2 and the calling of the woman by the name Eve in Genesis 3? Could this indicate that man did not dominate woman until after the fall? This interpretation is both compelling and intriguing.[64]

It is impossible to be dogmatic about the significance of the calling of woman in Genesis 2. There is simply not enough biblical evidence. But what is clear is the overwhelming emphasis on the mutuality of the first couple.

There is no statement of woman's inferiority in the first two chapters of Genesis. This has to be read into the text. Neither is there any hint in these accounts of creation that Eve reflected less of her creator. Man was not created superior. There was no discrimination in creation.

But this does not mean that man and woman are the same. It is just as wrong to insist on the sameness of the sexes or on an androgynous beginning as it is to argue for the superiority of the male. Sexual differentiation existed from the beginning.

The Bible neither absolutizes nor relativizes sexual differentiation. Sexuality is important, but second in importance to the fact that man and woman are made in God's image. The primary relationship is with God. Sexual differentiation is kept in perspective when we bear in mind that both sexes are made in God's image.

Adam and Eve were created in God's image and shared the same place in the created order. They were made of the same essence and created for unity. They resembled each other more than they resembled any other creature, but they were not mirror images of each other. As well as unity there was diversity in their relationship. This differentiation means that the sexes complement and correspond to each other. This is a beautiful picture. The unity, diversity and complementarity of the man and the woman mirrored the unity, diversity and complementarity of the Trinity in whose image they were made.

Sadly, this harmony was soon to be disrupted.

Notes

1 J. A. Phillips, *Eve: The History of an Idea* (Harper and Row, 1984), p. xiii.

2 On the history of Eve in Western culture see Phillips, *Eve.*

3 Phillips, *Eve*, especially chs. 6 and 11.

4 For a longer discussion see M. J. Evans, *Woman in the Bible* (Paternoster, 1983), pp. 14–7.

5 See especially 1 Cor. 11:3–16; 1 Tim. 2:9–15.

6 For an example of the egalitarian interpretation see P. H. Jewett, *Man as Male and Female* (Eerdmans, 1975).

7 J. Milton, *Paradise Lost* (Oxford University Press, 1958), Book 8, lines 541–5446.

8 J. O'Faolain and L. Martines (eds.), *Not in God's Image: Women in History* (Virago, 1979).

9 Augustine, *On the Holy Trinity*, trans. A. W. Haddan and W. G. T. Shedd, *Select Library of the Nicene and Post-Nicene Fathers*, vol. III (Eerdmans, 1956), p. 159.

10 Augustine, *On the Holy Trinity*, pp. 524–5.

11 Thomas Aquinas, *Summa Theologica*, trans. Fathers of the English Dominican Province (22 volumes, London, 1921–32), IV, part 1, XCIII, 4.

12 J. Calvin, *A Commentary on Genesis* (Banner of Truth, 1975), p. 129.

13 Quoted in M. Potter, 'Gender Equality and Gender Hierarchy in Calvin's Theology', *Signs: Journal of Women in Culture and Society*, vol. 11, no. 4.

14 Quoted in Potter, 'Gender Equality'.

15 D. Spender, *Man-Made Language* (Routledge and Kegan Paul, 1980), p. 166.

16 Plato relates the ancient Greek myth of Androgyne in the *Symposium.* Philo (d. *c.* AD 50) took up the idea and tried to understand Genesis 1:26 in this way. There has been a tendency in Eastern Christianity to see sexual differentiation as the result of the fall. Nicholas Berdayaev (1874–1948), the Russian orthodox theologian, is a well-known exponent of this view.

17 R. R. Ruether, *New Woman, New Earth* (Seabury Press, 1975), p. 26.

18 For a discussion of the way that thinkers absolutize or relativize sexual differentiation see H. Blocher, *In the Beginning* (IVP, 1984), p. 101.

19 How does sexual differentiation relate to man and woman being made in the image of God? The traditional understanding is expressed by G. C. Berkouwer, *Man: The Image of God* (IVP, 1962), p. 73: 'It is true that "God created man in his own image" is followed immediately by "male and female he created them". But this does not necessarily mean that the second clause gives a definition of the first; it does not necessarily imply that the image of God lies in the relationship between man and woman.'

Barth was the first to ground human sexuality in the image. He argues that 'Man in the image of God is Man as male and female.' Jewett, in *Man as Male and Female*, pp. 35–50, develops this idea of Barth's. Unlike Barth, Jewett rejects the hierarchical view of the relationship between the sexes.

J. Stott, *Issues Facing Christians Today* (Marshall Pickering, 1984), pp. 237–8, seems to offer the most balanced interpretation: 'We must be careful not to speculate beyond what the text warrants. Yet, if both sexes bear the image of God (as is forcefully asserted), then this seems to include not only our humanity (authentic humanness reflecting divinity), but our plurality (our relationships of love reflecting those which unite the persons of the Trinity) and even, at least in the broadest sense, our sexuality.'

20 Some theologians have argued that the use of the two words 'image' and 'likeness' is significant and they have made a distinction between the two terms. There is now general agreement that the two words are interchangeable (*cf.* Gn. 5:1–3 which uses both words alternately); see Berkouwer, *Man*, pp. 67–9.

21 For summaries of the ways the image has been understood see Berkouwer, *Man*, pp. 69–119, and Blocher, *In the Beginning*, pp. 80–2. The image has been understood in the following ways: (1) The image refers to spirituality: conformity to the image of Christ. (2) The image refers to dominion: humanity is in the image of God as God's representatives on earth. (3) The image is in the relationship of male and female (see note 19 above). It is clear from several passages that, though marred, man and woman remain in God's image after the fall (Gn. 9:6; 1 Cor. 11:7; Jas. 3:9).

22 John Chrysostom, *Quales ducendae sint uxores*, quoted in S. B. Clark, *Man and Woman in Christ* (Servant Books, 1980), p. 292.

23 Calvin, *Genesis*, p. 96.

24 Quoted in O'Faolain and Martines (eds.), *Not in God's Image*, p. 208.

25 *Luther's Works*, vol. 54, *Tabletalk*, ed. and trans. T. G. Tappert (Fortress Press, 1967), p. 8.

26 A. Trollope, *Phineas Finn* (1896: Penguin, 1972), p. 328.

27 E. C. Stanton (ed.), *The Woman's Bible* (1895: Polygon, 1985), pp. 15–6.

28 J. B. Hurley, *Man and Woman in Biblical Perspective* (IVP, 1981), pp. 207–9. Hurley compares the position of Adam, the first-formed, with that of Christ, the firstborn over all creation, and thus exaggerates Adam's privileges.

29 Philo of Alexandria (*c.* 20 BC – AD 50), quoted in Phillips, *Eve*, p. 30.

30 *E.g.* P. Trible, *God and the Rhetoric of Sexuality* (Fortress, 1978), p. 102.

31 Stanton (ed.), *The Woman's Bible*, Part I, p. 19.

32 Trible, *Rhetoric*, p. 141.

33 Clark, *Man and Woman*, p. 16.

34 1 Cor. 11:8–9; 1 Tim. 2:13.

35 Blocher, *In the Beginning*, p. 96.

36 Clement, *Pedagogue* 3.10, quoted in Clark, *Man and Woman*, p. 288–9.

37 Clement, *Stromata* 3.12, quoted in Clark, *Man and Woman*, p. 289

38 Augustine, *The City of God*, Book 12, trans. H. Bettenson (Penguin, 1980), pp. 503–4; Aquinas, *Summa Theologica*, quoted in S. T. Foh, *Women and the Word of God* (Presbyterian and Reformed Publishing Co., 1979), p. 60.

39 Calvin, *Genesis*, p. 131.

40 J. Calvin, *Commentary on the First and Second Epistles of Paul the Apostle to Timothy*, trans. T. A. Smail (1556: Oliver and Boyd, 1964), pp. 217–8.

41 For a further discussion see Blocher, *In the Beginning*, p. 104, and Trible, *Rhetoric*, p. 90.

42 Other examples are Ex. 18:4; Dt. 33:7; Pss. 27:9; 33:20; 94:17; 115:9–11; 124:8.

43 Quoted in L. M. Russell (ed.), *Feminist Interpretations of the Bible* (Basil Blackwell, 1985), p. 106.

44 Quoted in Phillips, *Eve*, p. 29.

45 Quoted in Phillips, *Eve*, p. 29.

46 For fuller discussion see R. R. Ruether, *Religion and Sexism* (Simon and Schuster, 1974), pp. 156–7.

47 Augustine, *City of God*, Book 12, p. 1057.

48 Karl Barth allegorizes in the same way in *The Doctrine of Creation* (T. and T. Clark, 1958), p. 321.

49 M. Henry, *Commentary on the Whole Bible*, vol. 1 (1706: MacDonald Publishing Co., no date), p. 19.

50 Stanton (ed.), *The Woman's Bible*, Part I, p. 20.

51 Blocher, *In the Beginning*, p. 101.

52 P. Trible, in 'De-patriarchalizing in Biblical Interpretation', *Journal of the American Academy of Religion*, 41 (1973), p. 37, says: 'Man has no part in making woman . . . He exercises no control over her existence. He is neither participant nor spectator nor consultant at her birth. Like man, woman owes her life solely to God. For both of them the origin of life is a divine mystery.'

53 C. de Pizan, *The Book of the City of Ladies*, trans. E. J. Richards (Persea Books, 1982), p. 23.

54 M. Hayter, in *The New Eve in Christ* (SPCK, 1987), p. 99, says: 'No indication of female subordination is contained in the use of the word 'issa, it is simply a Hebraic figure of speech. 'Issa is "taken

out of" 'is, but so is 'adam taken out of 'damah, "earth", and 'adam is not portrayed as a supernumerary addition to the earth nor as subordinate to it . . . What, after all, could be more humbling than to be told that one was made out of the dust?'

55 Calvin, *Genesis*, p. 133.

56 On this interpretation see Blocher, *In the Beginning*, pp. 99–100.

57 Blocher, *In the Beginning*, p. 96.

58 L. Scanzoni and N. Hardesty, *All We're Meant to Be* (Word Books, 1974), p. 26.

59 D. L. Sayers, *Are Women Human?* (IVP, USA, 1971), p. 37.

60 On this interpretation see Hurley, *Man and Woman*, p. 210, and Clark, *Man and Woman*, p. 26.

61 *E.g.* Gn. 32:28.

62 Trible, *Rhetoric*, pp. 99–100.

63 Trible, *Rhetoric*, pp. 99–100.

64 For a fuller discussion see Hayter, *New Eve*, pp. 100–1.

CHAPTER FIVE

Scoring points from Genesis 3

The cruel myth of Eve's guilt has succeeded in its purpose. The Christian Church has used it for 2,000 years to chasten women, and women themselves have accepted it as proof of their unworthiness. This gigantic hoax was perpetrated by men with the deliberate intention of placing women in a subservient, penitential and guilt-ridden position.[1]

THERE is considerable truth in Elizabeth Gould Davies' accusation. Genesis 3 has been consistently retold as a cautionary tale to keep women in their place. In this male-biased version of the story, the serpent approaches the woman first because she is the weaker and more gullible of the original pair. She succumbs to Satan's wiles and becomes his accomplice in seducing Adam to sin. Eve, the temptress, is judged more guilty than Adam, who sinned against his better judgment. She is punished more severely. The daughters of Eve, like her, are more susceptible to sin. They too must be chastened for the guilt of their foremother. Since women are more easily deceived and enticed into heresy, they are regarded with suspicion. They must be kept under strict control. The whole female sex is depreciated in this interpretation of Genesis.

Commentaries on Genesis 3 have succeeded in vilifying woman. But to what extent is Genesis 3 itself a commentary on the wicked wiles of women? Could it be that the commentators and exegetes have often been more negative than the text? Increasingly, the negative image of Eve is being questioned as a distinction is made between the male-biased interpretations of the text and the biblical narrative itself.[2]

Now the serpent was more crafty than any of the wild animals the LORD God had made. He said to the woman, 'Did God really say, "You must not eat from any tree in the garden"?'

The woman said to the serpent, 'We may eat fruit from the trees in the garden, but God did say, "You must not eat fruit from the tree that is in the middle of the garden, and you must not touch it, or you will die." '

'You will not surely die,' the serpent said to the woman. 'For God knows that when you eat of it your eyes will be opened, and you will be like God, knowing good and evil.'

When the woman saw that the fruit of the tree was good for food and pleasing to the eye, and also desirable for gaining wisdom, she took some and ate it. She also gave some to her husband, who was with her, and he ate it. Then the eyes of both of them were opened, and they realised that they were naked; so they sewed fig leaves together and made coverings for themselves.

Then the man and his wife heard the sound of the LORD God as he was walking in the garden in the cool of the day, and they hid from the LORD God among the trees of the garden. But the LORD God called to the man, 'Where are you?'

He answered, 'I heard you in the garden, and I was afraid because I was naked; so I hid.'

And he said, 'Who told you that you were naked?

Have you eaten from the tree from which I commanded you not to eat?'

The man said, 'The woman you put here with me – she gave me some fruit from the tree, and I ate it.'

Then the LORD God said to the woman, 'What is this you have done?'

The woman said, 'The serpent deceived me, and I ate.'

So the LORD God said to the serpent, 'Because you have done this,

> 'Cursed are you above all the livestock
> ` and all the wild animals!
> You will crawl on your belly
>> and you will eat dust
>> all the days of your life.
> And I will put enmity
>> between you and the woman,
>> and between your offspring and hers;
> he will crush your head,
>> and you will strike his heel.'

To the woman he said,

> 'I will greatly increase your pains in childbearing;
>> with pain you will give birth to children.
> Your desire will be for your husband,
>> and he will rule over you.'

To Adam he said, 'Because you listened to your wife and ate from the tree about which I commanded you, "You must not eat of it,"

> 'Cursed is the ground because of you;
>> through painful toil you will eat of it
>> all the days of your life.
> It will produce thorns and thistles for you,

and you will eat the plants of the field.
By the sweat of your brow
    you will eat your food
until you return to the ground,
    since from it you were taken;
for dust you are
    and to dust you will return.'

Adam named his wife Eve, because she would become the mother of all the living.

The LORD God made garments of skin for Adam and his wife and clothed them. And the LORD God said, 'The man has now become like one of us, knowing good and evil. He must not be allowed to reach out his hand and take also from the tree of life and eat, and live for ever." So the LORD God banished him from the Garden of Eden to work the ground from which he had been taken. After he drove the man out, he placed on the east side of the Garden of Eden cherubim and a flaming sword flashing back and forth to guard the way to the tree of life. (Gn. 3:1–24)

Why Eve?

Why was the temptation directed at the woman first? A long tradition of interpretation depicts Eve as defective and more open to temptation. The Church Fathers took this line. Augustine, for example, wrote:

He [Satan] had deceitful conversation with the woman – no doubt starting with the inferior of the human pair so as to arrive at the whole by stages, supposing that the man would not be so easily gullible, and could not be trapped by a false move on his part, but only if he yielded to another's mistake.[3]

101

In the dualistic thinking of the Church Fathers, man equals the soul and rationality; woman equals the body and irrationality or sensuality. Woman is a symbol of weakness or the body in relation to the soul, man. She is therefore more carnal and liable to sin.[4]

Luther took up the theme of woman's frailty in his lectures on Genesis. He waxed eloquent on the superiority of man:

> The subtleness is observable also in this, that Satan attacks human nature where it is weakest: Eve, the woman, and not Adam, the man. For although both of them had been created equally righteous, Adam nevertheless excelled Eve. For, as in the rest of nature everywhere, the strength of the male exceeds the female, so the male somewhat excelled the female even when nature still was perfect. Therefore, Satan, seeing that Adam was the more excellent creature, did not dare attack him; for he was afraid that his attempt would fail. And I believe that if he had attacked Adam first, Adam would have gained the victory. He would have crushed the serpent with his foot and said: Hold your tongue! The Lord has commanded otherwise.[5]

Although Luther stood out courageously in his generation for the doctrine of *sola scriptura*, this conversation between Satan and Adam is pure fiction. The passage highlights the way that fact and fiction have been confused in interpreting Genesis 3. For there is no evidence in the text that Adam is less susceptible to sin than Eve.

Matthew Henry, writing in the eighteenth century, elaborated on the nature of Eve's weakness. He suggested that she was 'inferior to Adam in knowledge, and strength, and presence of mind'.[6] Henry was following a well-established tradition in portraying Eve as less resolute and rational than Adam. Umberto Cassuto, a modern commentator, attributes Eve's susceptibility to sin to her greater imagination. He suggests that 'in imagination the woman magnifies the effects of eating amazingly; possibly for the very reason that a woman's imagination surpasses a man's, it was the woman who was enticed first'.[7] So, over the centuries, Eve has been characterized as being irresolute, irrational, more sensual and open to temptation. She has been accused of being more curious, vain, insecure, greedy, and conspiratorial.[8]

Surprisingly, when we scrutinize Genesis 3 we find no clues as to why the serpent tempted Eve first. The account simply records the conversation between the serpent and the woman. But where the Bible is silent, generations of interpreters and commentators have been happy to fill in the details and expound the supposed moral frailty of the female sex. All of this is speculation. Perhaps the cleverness of the serpent lies more in his method of temptation with half-truths and slight distortions of God's command than in his choice of victim.[9]

Feminist theologians have attempted to relieve the impression of Eve's gullibility and frailty. The case for the defence rests on Eve's reply to the serpent which, it is claimed, proves she is 'intelligent, informed and perceptive'.[10] Eve may have been misunderstood and maligned, but no appeal to her intelligence can completely excuse her of her part in the first crime.

First to fall

Eve was the first to eat of the forbidden fruit, which she then offered to her husband. Does this make her more, or primarily, guilty of the first sin? The sex of the theologian often determines the way the blame is apportioned when interpreting Genesis 3. The most laudable motives have been attributed to both Adam and Eve. The contention of many modern feminist theologians is that the traditional interpretation reads like an anti-feminist tale. It is true that many Bible commentators have regarded Eve as the villain of the piece. For example, Tertullian of Carthage, in the context of vigorously denouncing the extravagant fashions of the women in his congregation, said:

> And do you not know that you are each an Eve? The sentence of God on this sex of yours lives in this age: the guilt must of necessity live too. You are the devil's gateway; you are the unsealer of that forbidden tree; you are the first deserter of the divine law; you are she who persuaded him whom the devil was not valiant enough to attack. You destroyed so easily God's image, man. On account of your desert – that is, death – even the Son of God had to die.[11]

Eve, according to Tertullian, bears primary responsibility for mankind's downfall. This interpretation is not confined to Christian tradition: a well-known Jewish saying in the book of Ecclesiasticus runs, 'From a woman sin had its beginning, and because of her we all die.'[12]

The impression of Eve's guilt is heightened by crediting her with all sorts of unworthy motives, whereas Adam is ingeniously excused and made to appear less culpable. Augustine, for example, accused her of 'a certain love of her own power and a certain proud self-presumption'.[13] Aquinas asserted that 'she is more puffed up than the man'.[14] For some, Eve's crime lay in exerting her independence over her husband. According to Calvin, unbelief is at the root of Adam and Eve's defection, but he held Eve particularly guilty for having 'perversely exceeded her proper bounds'.[15]

Adam is excused because, unlike Eve, he sins reluctantly, his motives are purer, and his guilt is less. Chrysostom pleaded for Adam because he 'transgressed not captivated by appetite, but merely from the persuasion of his wife'.[16] Augustine, likewise, justified Adam on the grounds that he yielded 'because they were so closely bound in partnership', and 'Adam refused to be separated from his only companion even if it involved sharing her sin'.[17]

Luther exonerated Adam 'because he was unwilling to distress the joy of his life, that is, his wife'. His fault was that 'he loved his wife more than he loved God'.[18] Milton expressed the traditional defence of Adam poetically when he claimed that Adam sinned 'against his better knowledge, not deceived. But fondly overcome with female charms . . . '[19]

This interpretation is still popular. The contemporary theologian Stephen B. Clark follows the same tradition when he explains away Adam's disobedience by suggesting that 'perhaps he simply wants to accommodate or please his wife'.[20] Cassuto, too, claims mitigating circumstances in Adam's case: 'In regard to the man, the Bible does not state his motives for eating, as it does in the case of the woman, since for him it suffices that she is the one who gives him the fruit. It is the way of the world for the man to be easily swayed by the woman.'[21]

The Genesis account has been subtly changed. Eve has become the *femme fatale* who sins because of some inherent flaw. Adam is the tragic hero who is led astray because of love for his wife. Unquestionably, Eve's guilt is greater.

Once Eve had become a seductress in the minds of interpreters, only a little imagination was required for the first sin to become sexual. The Church Fathers often equated original sin with sexual activity or sexual awareness. For example, Chrysostom wrote:

> Scarcely had they turned from obedience to God than they became earth and ashes, and all at once, they lost the happy life, beauty and honour of virginity: thereupon God took virginal chastity from them . . . then did marriage make its appearance . . . Do you see where marriage took its origin? For where there is death, there too is sexual coupling.[22]

Woman, sex, and death are inexorably linked in this interpretation of the fall.

This negative image of Eve permeates Western culture. For example, Western religious art, taking its cue from theology, has depicted Eve as the traitress and temptress, the one who became Satan's accomplice in overthrowing Adam. In fact, woman was so closely associated with sin

Michelangelo, *The Temptation* (1511), Sistine Chapel, Vatican. The serpent and the woman are allied. An unmistakably female serpent, half woman, half snake, tempts Adam and Eve. They take the fruit from the tree of knowledge which in this painting is a fig tree – the fig being symbolic of lust.

and Satan that it became quite common in medieval art
for the serpent to appear as a female or for Satan to be
portrayed as a mirror image of Eve. There are numerous
examples of this. Michelangelo's serpent on the ceiling of
the Sistine Chapel in Rome is unmistakably female, as is

Façade of Notre-Dame, Paris, north door (twelfth century). A
female serpent tempts the original couple.

Le paradis terrestre from The Limbourg brothers, *Très Riches Heures du Duc de Berry* (early fifteenth century), Musée Condé, Chantilly. The likeness of the serpent to Eve is striking. Satan and the woman have become indistinguishable as accomplices. (Giraudon)

Jean Cousin le père (1490–1560), *Eva Prima Pandora*, Musée du Louvre, Paris. This is the classic image of woman as the source of evil. The Greek myth of Pandora and the biblical account of Eve have been fused to produce 'Eve the first Pandora'. Eve's left hand rests on the jar from which she has released all the ills of the world. A serpent coils around the same arm. Her right hand holds the forbidden fruit. She rests on a skull since she alone is responsible for the entry of death into the world. (© Photo R.M.N.)

the one that tempts Adam and Eve on the façade of Notre-Dame Cathedral in Paris. In one of the most famous of books of hours, that of the Duc de Berry, Adam and Eve are confronted by a flaxen-haired serpent who is the mirror image of Eve. This association of the woman with evil and Satan is so complete that when the French sculptor Rodin depicted the hand of the devil, the hand inevitably holds out a woman.

Sometimes biblical and mythological traditions were confused and synthesized. So Jean Cousin painted Eve as the 'prima Pandora', the one who, like the mythological Pandora, alone bears responsibility for the ills of the world.

The memory of Eve the temptress is still with us. She often reappears in modern cartoons and advertisements. The powerful image of Eve proffering the forbidden fruit is still irresistibly attractive.

A masterpiece of male manipulation

Women have reacted angrily to the character defamation of Eve. Dale Spender writes: 'Rather than blaming the man for his weakness in yielding to temptation, the woman is branded as a dangerous, irresistible temptress . . . a masterpiece of male manipulation.'[23]

Others have been anxious to clear Eve's name by discovering plausible motives for her behaviour or by shifting the blame on to Adam. Judith Murray, writing at the end of the eighteenth century, provided an early feminist defence of Eve. In her essay on 'The Equality of the Sexes' (1790), she excused Eve, arguing that Eve was motivated by a desire to adorn her mind and quench her thirst for intellectual knowledge. It was 'a laudable ambition which fired her soul'.[24] But Murray could discover no excuse for Adam's behaviour. Adam could see the results of Eve's disobedience, and that she had not gained the wisdom she had hoped to obtain, but he deliberately disobeyed God in spite of this. Murray therefore finds him the more guilty. A century later, Lillie Devreux Blake, one of the contributors to *The Woman's Bible*, argued polemically that Adam was more guilty than Eve.

Reading this narrative carefully, it is amazing that any set of men ever claimed that the dogma of the inferiority of woman is here set forth. The conduct of Eve from the beginning to the end is so superior

110

to that of Adam . . . Then the woman, fearless of death if she can gain wisdom, takes of the fruit; and all this time Adam standing beside her interposes no word of objection . . . Had he been the representative of the divinely appointed head in married life, he assuredly would have taken upon himself the burden of the discussion with the serpent, but no, he is silent in this crisis of their fate. Having had the command from God himself, he interposes no word of warning or remonstrance, but takes the fruit from the hand of his wife without a protest. It takes six verses to describe the fall of woman, the fall of man is contemptuously dismissed in a line and a half.

The subsequent conduct of Adam was to the last degree dastardly. When the awful time of reckoning comes, and the Jehovah God appears to demand why his command has been disobeyed, Adam endeavours to shield himself behind the gentle being he has declared to be so dear. 'The woman thou gavest to be with me, she gave me and I did eat,' he whines – trying to shield himself at his wife's expense! Again we are amazed that upon such a story men have built up a theory of their superiority![25]

More recently Phyllis Trible has defended Eve by arguing that despite the allegations of many interpreters Genesis does not provide evidence that Eve tempted Adam. She compares Adam unfavourably with Eve because he did not reflect on, theologize about or envisage the consequences of his action. According to her summing up of the events in the garden, 'his one act is belly-oriented, and it is an act of acquiescence, not of initiative. If the woman is intelligent, sensitive and ingenious, the man is passive, brutish, and inept.'[26]

The defence of Eve is often based on as few facts as the case against her. It is right to insist on Adam's guilt, but often the evidence against him is exaggerated. Mary Hayter, a contemporary theologian, gives a more measured response to the traditional interpretation of Eve's guilt. 'If the man was so strong that he was unsusceptible to temptation, he would have obeyed God in spite of the woman's perfidy.'[27] She has a point. It took the might of Satan to overcome Eve, whereas Adam succumbed to the suggestion of a mere woman.

Partners in crime

> Thus, they in mutual accusation spent
> The fruitless hours, but neither self-condemning,
> And of thir vain contest appeerd no end.[28]

When God questioned Adam and Eve about their disobedience, Adam blamed Eve and she blamed the serpent. Men and women have been displaying the same reactions ever since. The game of scoring points from Genesis 3 goes on as each sex attempts to make the other appear more guilty or to shift the blame. The fact remains that they were both found guilty. The superiority of one sex over the other can be established only by manipulating the evidence and misreading the text.

Adam and Eve both shared in the first crime. They were both asked to explain themselves, and both were held responsible for their actions. Adam was questioned first and then Eve. Eve's guilt is clearly not regarded as being primary or even greater than Adam's. Elsewhere in the Bible, Adam's personal guilt is stated very explicitly.[29] All we are told about the difference between Adam's sin and Eve's is that Eve was deceived whereas Adam was not.[30]

Adam and Eve's motivation in giving in to Satan's temptation is not absolutely clear. They may both have been tempted by the idea of being like God, but we cannot be sure. What is certain is that their sin was not essentially directed against each other but against God. They sinned as they broke God's command; they were both equally guilty of this disobedience. Eve did not sin primarily by taking the lead or exalting herself above her husband, but she sinned in exalting herself to question and break God's command.[31] Nor is there any indication that the original sin was sexual. Sexual union took place in Genesis 2, before the fall and at the command of God. The disobedience of Adam and the disobedience of Eve were almost simultaneous. It was only after Adam had eaten of the fruit that 'the eyes of both of them were opened'. They fell as one.

Death penalty

Commentators who have judged Eve to be more guilty have inevitably sentenced her more severely. Calvin, for example, gave the following verdict:

> Woman is more guilty than the man, because she was seduced by Satan, and so diverted her husband from obedience to God that she was an instrument of death leading all to perdition. It is necessary that woman recognise this, and that she learn to what she is subjected; and not only against her husband. This is reason enough why today she is placed below and that she bears within her ignominy and shame.[32]

In his commentary on Genesis he argued in very strong language: 'Thus the woman who had perversely exceeded her proper bounds is forced back to her own position . . . she is cast into servitude.'[33] According to Calvin, then, Eve received her just deserts: she sinned by exerting her independence of her husband; the punishment to fit this crime was to be harshly subject to him.

Luther made a similar pronouncement:

> Now there is added to these sorrows of gestation

113

and birth that Eve has been placed under the power of her husband . . . This punishment, too, springs from original sin; and the woman bears it just as unwillingly as she bears those pains and inconveniences that have been placed upon her flesh. The rule remains with her husband, and the wife is compelled to obey him by God's command. He rules the home and the state, wages wars, defends his possessions, tills the soil, builds, plants, etc. The woman, on the other hand, is like a nail driven into the wall. She sits at home . . . Just as the snail carries its household with it, so the wife should stay at home and look after the affairs of the household, as one who has been deprived of the ability of administering those affairs that are outside and concern the state. She does not go beyond her most personal duties . . .

Women are generally disinclined to put up with this burden, and they naturally seek to gain what they have lost through sin. If they are unable to do more, they at least indicate their impatience through grumbling. However, they cannot perform the functions of men: teach, rule, etc. In procreation and in feeding and nurturing their offspring they are masters. In this way Eve is punished; but as I said at the beginning it is a gladsome punishment if you consider the hope of eternal life and the honour of motherhood which have been left her.[34]

Luther was echoing a traditional interpretation of Genesis 3 when he emphasized the positive aspects of Eve's punishment. Generations of commentators have maintained that servitude is a gift of God,[35] and that it is 'a gladsome punishment' for the woman. These interpretations strike horror into the hearts of women. What could be worse than being 'cast into servitude' or 'a nail driven into the wall'? It appears that God has sanctioned the worst forms of male oppression and has sided with man against woman. Has this double standard been given divine sanction?

A student once remarked to me, 'I cannot help blaming God a little bit for putting women in a position where they will always be losers.' Women have certainly been losers throughout history. But we should not blame God; it was not his idea. His original purpose was that man and woman should live together without discord. Man's rule over woman is listed among the other tragic consequences of the fall in Genesis 3. In this context man's rule is clearly not one of God's blessings. Those who argue that male domination is a blessing would also (to be consistent) have to say that thorns and thistles, toil and sweat, disease and death, are blessings too. But the statements in Genesis 3 regarding woman have always been applied with greater severity than they warrant. Until quite recently, it was considered wrong to relieve pain in childbirth because it was taken to be the will of God that women should suffer. As well as being cruel, this was illogical and based on a selective reading of the text.

God has not given his blessing to male exploitation of women. A man's right to rule brutally is not established by divine decree. Elsewhere in the Bible it is very obvious that wife-beating is not God's idea. Men are commanded to be 'considerate', to 'love their wives', and not to 'be harsh with them'.[36]

Genesis 3 describes and predicts the inevitable results of banishment from God's presence. At the same time as man and woman were alienated from God they were alienated from each other. They hid from God, and they hid their nakedness from each other. Genesis 3 marks the beginning of the power struggle between the sexes. 'The created complementarity of one to the other will now be perverted into the rule of one over the other.'[37] Unity and harmony were replaced by disunity and disharmony. The Hebrew word *mashal*, usually translated 'rule', is a very strong word implying domination. The husband's rule will involve conflict or compulsion.[38] He will tyrannize and abuse his wife.

From this moment the world was weighted in man's favour.

The woman was told that her desire would be for her husband. This has commonly been interpreted in two ways: either as the desire to be ruled, resulting in clinging dependence and passivity, or as the desire to rule and dominate. The implication, however, is clear enough. Conflict and estrangement will become inevitable in the relationship between the sexes.

In passing judgment on the first couple, God punished them equally severely. They were both sentenced to 'hard labour'.[39] Exactly the same word is used in verses 16 and 17, though it is usually translated as 'pain' in verse 16 (in the judgment of the woman) and 'toil' in verse 17 (in the judgment of the man). The fruit of the body and the fruit of the earth will now be produced only by hard labour, pain and toil. In addition, for their part in the first crime, they were both sentenced to death. We are left in no doubt about the seriousness of their offence.

Writers and painters have often tried to capture the awfulness of this moment as Adam and Eve were expelled from the garden. They were driven from God's presence, out of Eden, never to return. Ahead lay a life of pain, suffering, and ultimately death. How they must have longed to return. Throughout history men and woman have shared this nostalgic longing for a time when things were not as bad as they are at the present. The response has been to try to recreate terrestrial paradises. All political and philosophical utopias could be interpreted in this light – as attempts to regain paradise lost. The women's movement is, in many ways, yet another pursuit of paradise. In designing feminist utopias women are trying to rediscover the liberty that was forfeited so long ago when man and woman were first exiled from God's presence.

Notes

1 E. G. Davies, *The First Sex* (Penguin, 1975), p. 144.

2 *E.g.* M. Hayter, *The New Eve in Christ* (SPCK, 1987), pp. 81–118.

3 Augustine, *The City of God*, trans. H. Bettenson (Penguin, 1980), p. 570.

4 For a fuller discussion of patristic theology see R. R. Ruether, *Religion and Sexism* (Simon and Schuster, 1974), pp. 150–1.

5 *What Luther Says, An Anthology*, vol. 3, compiled by E. M. Plass, (Concordia Publishing House, 1959), ref. 4129, p. 1290.

6 M. Henry, *Commentary on the Whole Bible* (1706: MacDonald Publishing Co., no date), pp. 21–2.

7 U. Cassuto, *A Commentary on the Book of Genesis*. Part One: *From Adam to Noah* (Magnes Press, 1961), p. 147.

8 For a fuller discussion see J. A. Phillips, *Eve, The History of an Idea* (Harper and Row, 1984), pp. 55–77.

9 This interpretation is supported by S. T. Foh, *Women and the Word of God* (Presbyterian and Reformed Publishing Co., 1979), p. 63.

10 P. Trible, *God and the Rhetoric of Sexuality* (Fortress, 1978), p. 110.

11 Tertullian, *De cultu feminarum* 1:1, *The Ante-Nicene Fathers*, vol. IV (Eerdmans, 1956), p. 14.

12 Ecclus. 25:24.

13 Augustine, *Genesis* xi.xxx, quoted in Phillips, *Eve*, p. 59.

14 Thomas Aquinas, *Summa Theologica* II, clxiii, 4, quoted in Phillips, *Eve*, p. 59

15 J. Calvin, *A Commentary on Genesis* (Banner of Truth, 1975), p. 172.

16 John Chrysostom, *Homily IX on Timothy*, *A Select Library of the Nicene and Post-Nicene Fathers*, vol. XIII (Eerdmans, 1956), p. 436.

17 Augustine, *City of God*, p. 570.

18 *What Luther Says*, vol. 3, ref. 4128, p. 1290.

19 J. Milton, *Paradise Lost*, Book 9, lines 998–9.

20 S. B. Clark, *Man and Woman in Christ* (Servant Books, 1980), p. 30.

21 Cassuto, *Genesis*, Part One, p. 148.

22 John Chrysostom, *Della Virginita*, quoted in J. O'Faolain and L. Martines (eds.), *Not in God's Image* (Virago, 1979), pp. 150–1.

23 D. Spender, *Man-Made Language* (Routledge and Kegan Paul, 1980), p. 168.

24 Quoted in D. Spender, *Women of Ideas (and What Men have Done to Them)* (Ark, 1982), p. 121.

25 L. D. Blake, 'Comments on Genesis', in E. C. Stanton (ed.), *The Woman's Bible* (1895: Polygon, 1985), pp. 26–7.

26 Trible, *Rhetoric*, p. 113.

27 Hayter, *New Eve*, p. 104.

28 J. Milton, *Paradise Lost*, Book 9, lines 1187–9.

29 Rom. 5:14.

30 2 Cor. 11:3; 1 Tim. 2:14.

31 For a fuller discussion see Foh, *Women and the Word*, p. 64.

32 Quoted in M. Potter, 'Gender Equality and Gender Hierarchy in Calvin's Theology', *Signs: Journal of Women in Culture and Society*, vol. 11, no. 4.

33 Calvin, *Genesis*, p. 172.

34 Quoted in Phillips, *Eve*, p. 105.

35 For a fuller discussion see D. Field, 'Headship in Marriage: the Husband's View', in S. Lees (ed.), *The Role of Women* (IVP, 1984), p. 47.

36 1 Pet. 2:7; Col. 3:19.

37 J. Stott, 'Man, Woman and the Bible' recorded lecture, London Institute of Contemporary Christianity.

38 On this interpretation see Clark, *Man and Woman*, pp. 33f.

39 On this interpretation see Hayter, *New Eve*, p. 107.

CHAPTER SIX

Perspectives on patriarchy

WHAT happened to the first couple after their expulsion from Eden? The Old Testament catalogues the history of Adam and Eve and their descendants. It makes disconcerting reading as far as women are concerned, for once man and woman were exiled from God's presence man gained the ascendancy. One of the results of alienation from God is that man and woman are alienated from one another. Parts of the Old Testament vividly illustrate the way aggression and deceit characterize relationships between sinful men and women.[1] The world is no longer as God intended it to be.

This raises a host of questions about the biblical attitude to women. Does God give his blessing to all the acts of brutality perpetrated against women in the Old Testament? Are women invisible and marginal in the history of Israel? Does Old Testament imagery denigrate women? Are they under male ownership? Does Old Testament religion devalue women as unclean and exclude them from the worship of Yahweh?

Women abused

Judges 19 – 20 describes a horrific incident of sexual violence. A Levite and his concubine arrived in Gibeah at dusk and an old man took them in for the night. They ate and drank, and then, while they were enjoying themselves, some wicked men of the city surrounded the house, pounded on the door and demanded to have sex with the Levite. The old man offered them his own daughter and the concubine. The men refused to listen, so the Levite sent his concubine outside to them. They raped and abused her throughout the night and at dawn let her go. She died in the doorway of the house with her hands on the threshold.

Elizabeth Cady Stanton, commenting on the terrible fate of the concubine, wrote: 'There are many instances in the Old Testament where women have been thrown to the mob, like a bone thrown to dogs, to pacify their passions; and women suffer today from these lessons of contempt, taught in a book so revered by the people.'[2]

Does the Bible teach that woman is no more than a bone to be thrown to dogs, as Elizabeth Cady Stanton implies? If it does, no wonder so many women have turned their backs in disgust on the church. But I do not believe that it does. After the fall, the world is largely under man's rule. Many Old Testament narratives depict the hard realities for women living in a world dominated by sinful men. But the Bible does not endorse all the behaviour that it records. The Old Testament does not always describe an ideal society reflecting God's purposes; it often describes a sinful society in rebellion against God. The chapters at the end of Judges portray a society which had abandoned the worship of God and was in a state of moral collapse. Everyone did what was right in his own eyes. The concubine's gruesome murder was symptomatic of the lawlessness of Israel. If a lesson is to be learned from the fate of the Levite's concubine, it is that when men are alienated from God, violence and depravity will result.

The book of Judges also includes the story of Jephthah, the warrior who vowed to the Lord as he went into battle that 'If you give the Ammonites into my hands, whatever comes out of the door of my house to meet me when I return in triumph from the Ammonites will be the LORD's, and I will sacrifice it as a burnt offering.' On his return his daughter, his only child, came out to meet him. She requested two months to roam the hills and weep with her friends because she would never marry. When the period had elapsed, she returned to her father and 'he did to her as he had vowed' (Jdg. 11:29–40).

There is some debate about whether Jephthah sacrificed his daughter or dedicated her to the Lord. Women are rightly outraged at the apparent sacrifice. But it is a mistake to suggest that God would condone such an act. The law of Moses expressly forbade child sacrifice. The people of Israel were told not to imitate the Canaanite religions which practised the burning of sons and daughters as part of the worship of their gods.[3] Jephthah tragically violated God's command if he offered his daughter as a burnt offering.[4]

As we read the Old Testament we have to distinguish between prescription and description. Prescriptive passages, such as the Ten Commandments, clearly reveal God's will; but descriptive passages, like the stories of the Levite's concubine or of Jephthah's daughter, may record Israel's faithlessness to God or an individual's folly and sin. We also have to take account of the different literary forms and cultural settings in the Old Testament. We are faced with great diversity, for the Old Testament includes historical narrative, proverbs, poetry and prophecy, and spans over a thousand years.

Women overlooked

The Old Testament is a man's book, where women appear for the most part as adjuncts of men, significant only in the context of men's activities.[5]

One way in which women are apparently depreciated in the Old Testament is by its man-centredness. It is often argued that in the historical narratives, while male characters are central to the plot, the women are either minor characters or ignored completely. The patriarchs are the dominant figures, and sons are more important than daughters. Women achieve significance as mothers of sons. Religious life generally revolves around men. Legally, women are dependants under the authority of their fathers or husbands, and rarely regarded in their own right. This is typical of a patriarchal culture.

It is a mistake, however, to assume that the Old Testament is the story of men's heroic exploits. It is the account of God's intervention in history and of the preparation of God's people for the coming of the Messiah. The purpose of the Old Testament is not to recall a golden age for men but to record God's dealings with Israel. The action revolves around the nation or the tribes. Understandably, therefore, national or tribal leaders tend to figure prominently. Men may be the central characters in the Old Testament but they are not models of virtue. Abraham is a liar, Jacob a cheat, Moses a murderer and David an adulterer. The Old Testament story describes the way God changed and shaped their lives.

Given the patriarchal background of the Old Testament, it is amazing that women appear so frequently within its pages. Women are not always banished into the background. Abigail, Esther, Hannah, Miriam, Naomi, Rachel, Rebekah, and Sarah are among those who played a role in the history of those times. Women of faith are on record as averting bloodshed, receiving back their dead raised to life, administering justice, and delivering the nation.[6] Women such as these who appear in the text have often been overlooked. Bad women have achieved notoriety; good ones have been forgotten. Everyone has heard of Jezebel and Delilah, but who knows of

Deborah and Huldah?

The most unlikely women make history. A poor widow, a servant girl in captivity, and midwives who feared God, are all singled out for mention.[7] God does not judge people according to sex or status but according to their faith. Both Rahab the prostitute and Ruth the Moabitess feature at length in the biblical records. Rahab was a prostitute in the Amorite city of Jericho when Joshua sent two spies to spy out the land (Jos. 2). She hid the two men and gave them inside information on the vulnerable state of Jericho. At the same time, Rahab declared her own belief that 'the LORD your God is God in heaven above and on the earth below' (Jos. 2:11). Courageously, Rahab stayed in Jericho until the Israelite army took the city. Later she married Salmon, a prince of Judah, and is named among the ancestors of Christ (Mt. 1:4–6).

Ruth, like Rahab, was not an Israelite. She was a Moabitess who had married an Israelite. When he died, she insisted on returning to Bethlehem with her mother-in-law, Naomi, who was also a widow. When Naomi tried to make her turn back, Ruth replied, 'Your people will be my people and your God my God' (Ru. 1:16). In Bethlehem Ruth was married again, to Boaz, and she too became an ancestor of Christ. Both Rahab and Ruth were women without men in a man's world; both were outsiders who did not belong to Israel; yet God honoured their faith. When women respond personally to God, their stories are recorded and they become visible in Old Testament history; otherwise they are included in the corporate life of Israel.

It is important to understand the corporate nature of Hebrew society, because this explains the apparent invisibility of women in Hebrew life. The individual's identity had meaning only within the corporate structure of the family, the tribe and the nation. Individuals identified themselves by referring to their 'father's house'.[8] Corporate identity was more important than personal identity. The husband or father was the unchallenged head of the family unit. Within this framework it was quite logical for the man to worship on behalf of his whole family, including both male and female family members. A Hebrew woman would have regarded herself as included in these religious acts. The corporate nature of society also explains why there was not always a clear distinction between a man, his belongings and his wife (Ex. 20:17).[9] Women were given in marriage by the head of the family, but it is wrong to assume that women were merely chattels. Marriages were arranged, but it is likely that women were consulted. Rebekah, for example, gave her consent to marrying Isaac (Gn. 24:1–66).

The ideal woman, according to the Old Testament, was a strong woman, 'clothed with strength and dignity' (Pr. 31:25). She was praised above everything else because she feared God (Pr. 31:30). A good wife was highly honoured; she was considered to be a gift from God, 'her husband's crown' and 'worth far more than rubies' (Pr. 19:14; 12:4; 31:10). Apart from bearing and raising children, the ideal Old Testament woman directed her household. Her sphere of activity does not appear to have been narrowly restricted and may have extended well beyond the confines of her own home (Pr. 31). Within a family the husband was the ruler, and the wife was under his authority. This did not mean, however, that a wife took no initiative or responsibility. The picture of the ideal wife in Proverbs 31 suggests just the opposite. She is a very strong, competent individual and is engaged in a wide range of commercial and charitable activities. Not only does she manage a large household; 'she considers a field and buys it . . . plants a vineyard . . . sets about her work vigorously . . . sees that her trading is profitable . . . opens her arms to the poor . . . speaks with wisdom and faithful instruction'. The most significant fact about this remarkable woman is her relationship to God; this is the source of her strength.

There are numerous examples of wives who appear to have made their own decisions. Hannah, for example, appears to have acted independently when she vowed to dedicate her firstborn to the service of God. Her vow was to have implications for the whole nation, since Samuel played a decisive role as a prophet (1 Sa. 1:10–11). Abigail, said to be a woman of 'good judgment', took matters into her own hands when she went to intercept David to stop him revenging himself on her foolish husband Nabal (1 Sa. 25:3–42).

In Israelite society, women were valued for their child-bearing role, though in God's eyes spiritual fruitfulness always appears to be more important (Is. 54). Sons were preferred to daughters. The importance of male seed and the detailed records of male lines of descent have led some to the conclusion that 'woman is no more than a bearer of male children'.[10] The barren woman was stigmatized. She sometimes resorted to desperate measures, giving her husband to another woman, to ensure that he produced a son (Gn. 16). Several Old Testament narratives record God's intervention in giving a son to a childless woman.[11] This preoccupation with male children may be partly explained by taking into account the fact that Israel was waiting for the fulfilment of the promise of a Messiah.[12] The miraculous births of the Old Testament (Sarah giving birth to Isaac, Rebekah to Jacob and Esau, Rachel to Joseph, Manoah's wife to Samson, Hannah to Samuel)[13] may have helped to prepare God's people mentally for the birth of the Messiah. The birth of Jesus was the culmination of the other miraculous births in the Old Testament.

As a mother, an Israelite woman commanded honour and respect. Children were directed to honour both father and mother (Ex. 20:12). The punishment for attacking or cursing a father or mother was the same in both cases, death (Ex. 21:15, 17). The warning in Proverbs is very strong; 'If a man curses his father or mother, his lamp will be snuffed out in pitch darkness' (Pr. 20:20). Parents had a joint responsibility for rearing children. They both played an important role in their education. Children were obliged to observe carefully their instruction; the book of Proverbs admonishes: 'Keep your father's commands and do not forsake your mother's teaching. Bind them upon your heart for ever; fasten them around your neck' (Pr. 6:20–21).

Women devalued

> I find more bitter than death
> the woman who is a snare,
> whose heart is a trap
> and whose hands are chains. . . .
> I found one upright man among a thousand,
> but not one upright woman among them all.
>
> (Ec. 7:26, 28)

These verses from Ecclesiastes are often quoted as the most blatantly misogynist comment in the Bible. Add to this other warnings about the immoral woman, and imagery which depicts Israel as a harlot or an adulteress, and it may appear that the Old Testament gives a thoroughly demeaning impression of women. Were the Old Testament writers intent on denigrating the female sex? A closer reading reveals that they were not.

The writer of Ecclesiastes describes his own bitter experience, but his disillusioned verdict cannot be assumed to be the Bible's final word on women. He expresses his own jaundiced view of life. Later in the book he admits that it is possible to enjoy and love a woman (Ec. 9:9). Relationships between men and women are sometimes portrayed very positively in other parts of the Old Testament. The Song of Songs, for example, which is in the form of a poetic dialogue between two lovers, beautifully describes the mutuality of the sexes. The poet writes:

> . . . love is as strong as death,
> its jealousy unyielding as the grave.
> It burns like blazing fire,
> like a mighty flame.
> Many waters cannot quench love;
> rivers cannot wash it away. (Song 8:6–7)

It would be wrong to assume that biblical writers as a whole were biased in man's favour. Man and woman are sometimes compared, to man's detriment; the writer of Proverbs, for example, writes:

> A kind-hearted woman gains respect,
>   but ruthless men gain only wealth.
> (Pr. 11:16)

It is important to read apparently negative statements and imagery in context. The Old Testament writers vigorously denounced harlotry because of its association with the fertility cults, not because they were viciously demeaning women. In fact, they spoke out against male as well as female temple prostitutes (Dt. 23:17–18).

The relationship between God and his people is often depicted as a conjugal relationship, so that when Israel is spiritually unfaithful she is compared to an adulterous wife or a prostitute. But this does not imply that women are the sinful sex; men as well as women are explicitly found guilty of unfaithfulness and deserting God.[14]

By no means all the female imagery in the Old Testament is negative. In Proverbs wisdom is personified as a female figure. The writer advises:

> Do not forsake wisdom, and she will protect you;
>   love her, and she will watch over you.
> wisdom is supreme; therefore get wisdom.
>   Though it cost all you have, get understanding.
> (Pr. 4:6–7)

Female imagery is also used to describe God. In some striking passages God is compared to a mother, as we saw in chapter 2.

Women as property

> Women were regarded as an inferior species to be
> owned like cattle, an unclean creature incapable
> of participating in the mysteries of the worship of
> Yahweh.[15]

Are women an inferior species? The Mosaic laws may
suggest this, but they reflect the social structure of the
times. In Leviticus 27:3–4, for example, the value of an
adult male who wishes to free himself from a vow is set at
fifty shekels, while that of a female is only thirty shekels.
This is a realistic estimate of the economic resources of a
woman in ancient Israel; a woman was worth thirty shekels
in that culture. It does not mean that intrinsically, in God's
eyes, she is worth less than a man.

Apparently only a husband could initiate a divorce in
Old Testament times (Dt. 24:1–4).[16] Is this another case
of preferential treatment? Does a man have the right to
discard his wife like a piece of unwanted property? Not at
all. The aim of the legislation in Deuteronomy was to
prevent remarriage of a couple who previously divorced
and married other people; its aim was not to encourage
divorce. The divorce measures were intended to contain
the damage caused by broken relationships.

'Moses did not work in Utopia.'[17] Jesus demonstrated
that the law on divorce was given to regulate a situation
that was less than ideal. He said, 'Moses permitted you to
divorce your wives because your hearts were hard. But it
was not this way from the beginning' (Mt. 19:3–12). The
Old Testament, too, speaks out in very strong language
against divorce. God declares plainly, 'I hate divorce'
(Mal. 2:16). To some extent the laws reflect the cultural
situation in which they were formulated.[18]

The same was true of polygamy. The law acknowledged
that it existed, and regulated abuse of polygamous relationships, but it was never seen as ideal (Dt. 21:15). In fact

the historical writings describe very realistically the dismal failure of polygamy. Jealousy, rivalry and bitterness inevitably characterize a *ménage à trois* (Gn. 16:30).

One of the main objections to the Old Testament law is that it appears to regard women as property. The laws relating to sexual offences sometimes create this impression. Sexual relations with an engaged or married woman were punished by death (Dt. 22:22–24). It is often assumed that the reason for this was that the woman was considered to be another man's property. There may be an element of this, but it was not simply a case of an infringement of property rights. In the Assyrian law, violation of a virgin was punished by violating the offender's wife.[19] This was clearly a matter of property rights. The family whose daughter had been seduced retaliated by meting out the same treatment to another woman. The Old Testament mentality was very different; retribution of this sort was never endorsed. The sexual relationship itself was regarded as sacrosanct. Sexual relationships were treated very seriously; every sexual relationship had repercussions. Men were not free to take unattached women. If a man had sex with an unattached woman then he must marry her; if she was already married or engaged then both the adulterer and adulteress were put to death. In the case of rape of a betrothed woman the man alone was put to death (Dt. 22:25–27). When a slave girl who was betrothed was forced to sleep with a man, the man alone was punished, though in this case the punishment was not death (Lv. 19:20–22).

Wives were not bought and sold, though sons and daughters were sold into slavery. The law afforded some protection for women slaves. A woman could not be resold to foreigners. If she was married she could not be displaced by another woman and deprived of her food, clothing and marital rights (Ex. 21:7–10). The Old Testament assumed that women would be captured in war, but at the same time it regulated conduct towards these captives. Wives could not be sold or treated as slaves even if they had been taken in war (Dt. 21:10–14). The law afforded some protection to women who would otherwise have been powerless.

Contrary to popular belief, a widow was not inherited by her husband's brother as part of her dead husband's property. The levirate law required the brother of a dead man to marry his widow, if she was childless, to perpetuate the line of the dead brother (Dt. 25:5–10). The law assumed that the woman would want to marry her brother-in-law so that her husband's 'name will not be blotted out from Israel', but she was not forced to do so. The law was designed to protect a widow; she had the right to enlist the support of the elders of the town if her brother-in-law refused to marry her (Dt. 25:7–10). God has a particular concern for widows, orphans and aliens. There are very strong warnings against taking advantage of these vulnerable members of society (Ex. 22:22–24). The story of Tamar and Onan shows God intervening and killing a man who abuses a widow (Gn. 38).

Women were not viewed as mere property, but their legal position was different from and subordinate to that of men. A father had the right to nullify or confirm the vow of an unmarried daughter; similarly a husband might prevent a wife from making a pledge. But the vows taken by a widow or divorced woman were binding (Nu. 30:1–16). Presumably this was because the father or husband would have had to bear the consequences of any rash promises made by an unmarried daughter or a wife. But the law was not intended to prevent a woman taking on serious obligations before God.

Sons usually inherited their father's property as a means of ensuring that each tribe retained its own tribal land. When a man died without sons, his daughters inherited providing they married within their own tribe so that land was not passed from tribe to tribe (Nu. 27:1–11; 36:1–12).

Unclean women

According to the law, a woman was unclean during menstruation and after childbirth (Lv. 15:19–30; 12:1–8). After
the birth of a son a woman was unclean for seven days;
then she must wait thirty-three days to be purified. If she
gave birth to a daughter, a woman was unclean for two
weeks and must then wait sixty-six days to be purified. In
other words, the birth of a female child made the mother
doubly unclean. Does this mean that women's bodies are
unclean, impure and polluting? Is this why they were segre-
gated and kept out of the sanctuary? Do these laws dis-
criminate against women? Why is the birth of a daughter
more defiling than that of a son?

It is a mistake to suggest that these laws denigrate
femaleness. They feature in a long section dealing with
ritual uncleanness caused by childbirth, infectious skin dis-
eases and bodily emissions in both sexes. Men were subject
to equally rigorous ceremonial laws (Lv. 15:1–16). Sexual
intercourse, loss of blood and bodily discharges made both
men and women unclean. Female impurity due to menstruation or childbirth does not make women any more morally
deficient than men.

All these laws served as graphic illustrations to draw
attention to the recurring uncleanness and sinfulness of
both men and women since the fall. They were visual aids
which constantly recalled Israel's moral guilt before God.
As the people performed ceremonial cleansings and
brought offerings to make atonement, they anticipated the
coming of the Messiah, the final sacrifice for sin. The
sacrificial system revolved around the shedding of blood,
thus preparing people mentally for the Lamb of God who
would shed his blood for the remission of sins.

Blood was treated with enormous respect in the Levitical
laws because blood equals life (Lv. 17:11). Loss of blood
means death. Bleeding during menstruation or after childbirth therefore became very significant. It was loss of blood

which made a woman unclean. Was this because loss of blood symbolizes death?[20] The doubling of the length of purification time after the birth of a daughter is puzzling, though it may emphasize that in the future the female child will menstruate. Whatever the reason for this discrepancy it does not mean that the female child was more sinful. The sin offering after the days of purification were over was exactly the same whether the baby was a boy or a girl (Lv. 12:6–8).

Women excluded

Was the religion of the Old Testament strictly a male religion from which females were excluded? At first glance this appears to be the case. All the animals used in the main offerings were male and were usually offered by men. When the priesthood developed in Israel it was restricted to the sons of Aaron.[21] Only males bore the sign of the covenant, circumcision. Regulations for worship were generally addressed to men. Only the men were required to attend the three annual festivals (Ex. 23:14–17). However, this is not the complete picture. Women were much more involved in religious life than is sometimes suggested.

The exclusion of females was not total. Male animals without defects were stipulated for the burnt offering and sin offering, but for other offerings female as well as male animals were used.[22] As for the fact that the offerings were usually made by men, the head of a house often represented all the members of the household in worship, and women were thereby included in the act. Noah, for example, sacrificed on behalf of himself, his wife, his sons and their wives after the flood; it was a corporate act (Gn. 8:20). This sense of corporateness explains why, although women were not circumcised, they regarded themselves as part of the covenant community. Significantly, the command to 'circumcise your hearts' and the promise that 'the LORD your God will circumcise your hearts and the hearts of your descendants, so that you may love him with all your heart and with all your soul, and live' (Dt. 10:16; 30:6) were addressed to Israel as a whole. Women in Israel were explicitly included in covenant relationships (Dt. 29:9–15).

Although women were not required to attend festivals, they were sometimes present. According to later legislation, women were generally *expected* to attend the festivals. (Dt. 12:8–14; 16:11, 14).[23] Presumably it was their periodic uncleanness and numerous pregnancies that precluded any *obligation* to do so. Purely practical reasons may account for women's partial exclusion from worship. Evidently Hannah, for example, usually went with Elkanah to offer the annual sacrifice, but she was given the option about whether to attend. She decided not to accompany him while she was nursing Samuel (1 Sa. 1:3–5, 21–23).

Women assembled along with men and children to listen to the reading of the law so that they could learn to fear the Lord their God and 'follow carefully all the words of this law'.[24] A woman took her own offering to the priest to mark the end of her ceremonial uncleanness (Lv. 12:6–8; 15:19–30). Occasionally a woman is mentioned as offering a sacrifice. Hannah, for example, took the sacrifice to the Shiloh temple when she dedicated Samuel to the Lord (1 Sa. 1:24–28).

Women were very specifically included in some aspects of worship. They served at the entrance to the tent of meeting[25] and functioned as members of the temple choirs.[26] Women could also consecrate themselves by a special vow of separation to the Lord (Nu. 6).

At a personal level women related directly to God without an intermediary. They prayed and praised God. Rebekah, Rachel and Hannah petitioned and thanked God in prayer.[27] Miriam and Deborah celebrated God's deliverance in song.[28] Sometimes, God communicated directly with women. The angel of the Lord, for example, spoke to Hagar and Manoah's wife.[29]

Three women, Miriam, Huldah and Deborah, stand out as prophetesses in the history of Israel.[30] They were used by God to deliver, judge and speak in his name. Miriam played a part in the exodus, leading Israel with Moses and Aaron (Mi. 6:4). Huldah passed God's judgment on Judah for their neglect of the Book of the Law. In her case, it is interesting that King Josiah sent Hilkiah the high priest plus four other leading men to enquire of her. She replied to them by speaking authoritatively in the name of the Lord, the God of Israel.

Deborah was perhaps the most remarkable of the three women. She was both a prophetess and a judge. The book of Judges introduces her in the following way:

> Deborah, a prophetess, the wife of Lappidoth, was leading Israel at that time. She held court under the Palm of Deborah between Ramah and Bethel in the hill country of Ephraim, and the Israelites came to her to have their disputes decided. (Jdg. 4:4–5)

She was a woman of enormous influence. Judges 4–5 tells how Deborah was instrumental in delivering Israel from the grip of Canaanite oppression. She sent for Barak from Kedesh to give him God's command to muster ten thousand men of Naphtali and Zebulun at Mount Tabor. She went with Barak to Tabor and was the one who gave the order to go into battle, declaring, 'Go! This is the day the Lord has given Sisera into your hands. Has not the Lord gone ahead of you?' (Jdg. 4:14). It is difficult to find another Old Testament character who matches Deborah for resolution and unshakeable belief in God.

This tradition of prophetesses appears to have continued into New Testament times. When the baby Jesus was presented in the temple he was greeted by the prophetess Anna. 'She never left the temple but worshipped night and day, fasting and praying.' She gave thanks to God for the baby and 'spoke about the child to all who were looking forward to the redemption of Jerusalem' (Lk. 2:37–38).

It is sometimes suggested that women were allowed to function as prophetesses because no suitable men were available.[31] Similar arguments are used today about female missionaries. The presence of a prominent woman like Deborah in the Old Testament is a source of embarrassment to some commentators. Many attempts have been made to minimize her role or to explain her away. Deborah is sometimes caricatured as a particularly domineering woman, so that Barak becomes the real hero. Calvin argued that Deborah and Huldah were special cases. He explained that 'God doubtless wished to raise them on high to shame the men and obliquely to show them their slothfulness'.[32] There is no evidence to support this. Huldah, for example, prophesied during the same period as Jeremiah and Zephaniah; they could have been consulted in preference to her. Some theologians reason that the offices of prophetess and judge were civil rather than religious.[33] But in a theocracy like Israel it is difficult to make a strict division between civil and religious functions, especially as these prophetesses claimed to speak the words of the Lord.

Life outside Eden is hard for women. The Old Testament reflects the inequalities and double standards of the patriarchal cultures which form the background to the text. But male domination is not complete. The Old Testament is not just a man's book. Women are more visible within its pages, and are portrayed more positively, than is often assumed. Most importantly, the Old Testament betrays no double standard in the way women relate personally to God. Women may have been second-class members of society, but they were not spiritually second-class. Salvation is for both sexes. The coming of Jesus makes this even more explicit.

Notes

1 Jdg. 16; 2 Sa. 13.
2 E. C. Stanton (ed.), *The Woman's Bible*, Part II, p. 16.
3 Lv. 18:21; Dt. 12:31.
4 Some interpreters argue that Jephthah's daughter was 'devoted'

or given over to the Lord rather than put to death. For a discussion of possible interpretations see W. C. Kaiser, Jr., *Hard Sayings of the Old Testament* (IVP, USA, 1988), pp. 104–5.

5 P. Bird, 'Images of Women in the Old Testament', in R. R. Ruether (ed.), *Religion and Sexism* (Simon and Schuster, 1974), p. 41.

6 Jdg. 4:4–5, 6–23; 1 Sa. 25:3–42; 2 Ki. 4:8–36.

7 Ex. 1:15–20; 1 Ki. 17:7–24; 2 Ki. 5:2–3.

8 On the corporate identity of Israel see J. B. Hurley, *Man and Woman in Biblical Perspective* (IVP, 1981), pp. 33–4.

9 On corporate personality in the Old Testament, see M. J. Evans, *Woman in the Bible* (Paternoster, 1983), p. 23.

10 E. Figes, *Patriarchal Attitudes* (Faber and Faber, 1970), p. 39.

11 *E.g.* Gn. 21:1–7; 1 Sa. 1.

12 This interpretation is favoured by P. Jewett, *Man as Male and Female* (Eerdmans, 1975), p. 121.

13 Gn. 21:1–6; 25:21–26; 30:22–24; Jdg. 13; 1 Sa. 1.

14 Je. 34:4; Ho. 4:10–15.

15 Sheila Collins, quoted in S. T. Foh, *Women and the Word of God* (Presbyterian and Reformed Publishing Co., 1979), p. 50.

16 On divorce and sexual offence in the Old Testament see Hurley, *Man and Woman*, pp. 38–9.

17 H. Blocher, 'Les données bibliques', recorded lecture, Église du Tabernacle, Paris.

18 For a comparison of Assyrian, Babylonian and Israelite cultures see Hurley, *Man and Woman*, pp. 20–57.

19 Hurley, *Man and Woman*, p. 39.

20 Calvin, Bonar and Keil view these discharges as symbolizing sin and death. See G. J. Wenham, *Leviticus, (The New International Commentary on the Old Testament,* Hodder and Stoughton, 1979), p. 222.

21 Ex. 28:1–3; Lv. 21.

22 On the Hebrew ceremonial system see Foh, *Women and the Word*, pp. 79–80.

23 On this changing attitude to women, see M. Hayter, *The New Eve in Christ* (SPCK, 1987), p. 65.

24 Dt. 31:12; Ne. 8:2.

25 Ex. 38:8; 1 Sa. 2:22.

26 Ezr. 2:65; Ne. 7:67.

27 Gn. 25:22–23; 30:6, 22; 1 Sa. 1:10–17.

28 Ex. 15:20–21; Jdg. 5.

29 Gn. 16:7–13; Jdg. 13:3–5.

30 Ex. 15:20–21; 2 Ki. 22:14–20; Jdg. 4.

31 On the legitimacy of the ministry of prophetesses see Evans, *Woman in the Bible*, pp. 30–1.

32 Quoted in Foh, *Women and the Word*, p. 84.

33 On this interpretation see Hurley, *Man and Woman*, pp. 47–8.

CHAPTER SEVEN

How revolutionary was Jesus?

WHAT impact did the coming of Jesus make? The description of him in the gospels makes compelling reading. Everywhere he went, he made the headlines. People were prepared to die for him, or plotted to kill him; they rarely remained indifferent. His teaching was radical, his behaviour unconventional. He was accused of blasphemy, and of mixing with the wrong people, many of whom were women. These women joined his following, received important teaching, and witnessed miracles. They are visible throughout the gospel records.

The inclusion of women in Jesus' ministry is a fact that has often been overlooked. Tragically, it has been assumed that he was a man like any other man. Once, when I was leading a seminar on 'Women and Christianity' in a British university, a member of a sexual equality group launched into a tirade against Jesus. She hurled accusations at him: 'Jesus didn't teach women in the same way as he taught men; he didn't engage in dialogue with them . . . He relegated women to a passive role; he didn't encourage them to be active like the male disciples . . . He didn't send them out to spread the gospel.' In her final counterblast she declared, 'All the women were allowed to do was wash his feet.'

To appreciate the extent of women's involvement in Jesus' ministry, and to understand why his attitude to women created shockwaves, we have to look at the way he related to women in the gospel records.

Women on the move

One piece of evidence that deals the death-blow to the idea that Jesus encouraged women to be passive is an intriguing passage in Luke's record.

> After this, Jesus travelled about from one town and village to another, proclaiming the good news of the kingdom of God. The Twelve were with him, and also some women who had been cured of evil spirits and diseases: Mary (called Magdalene) from whom seven demons had come out; Joanna the wife of Chuza, the manager of Herod's household; Susanna; and many others. These women were helping to support them out of their own means. (Lk. 8:1–3)

This was revolutionary. Women left their homes, took to the road and followed Jesus. Professor Jeremias, writing about the social position of women in New Testament times, comments that this was 'an unprecedented happening in the history of that time. John the Baptist had already preached to women and baptized them; Jesus, too, knowingly overthrew custom when he allowed women to follow him.'[1] The Twelve were commissioned for a special purpose (Lk. 6:12–16), but the group around Jesus was often larger.[2] At one time, for instance, there were seventy-two (Lk. 10:1–23). Considering that first-century women were probably secluded or separated from men for most of their lives, the travelling group described by Luke is remarkable. Jesus also put himself in an economically dependent position as he allowed Mary, Joanna, Susanna and the others to provide for him out of their resources.

These women, like the male disciples, appear to have come from a variety of backgrounds. Joanna, one of those mentioned, came from Herod's court, the very seat of the opposition to Jesus, and her husband was a senior official. Yet she identified herself with a man who was regarded as a state traitor.

Matthew and Mark shed more light on the activities of these women followers. They report that many women were present at the crucifixion.[3] Mark adds, 'In Galilee these women had followed him and cared for his needs. Many other women who had come up with him to Jerusalem were also there' (Mk. 15:41). Piecing together the fragments of information, this group of women appear to have been more involved in Jesus' ministry when he was near to their homes in Galilee. Since Galilee was the centre of Jesus' ministry, this means that their involvement was considerable. Their role parallels that of the disciples who received teaching and cared for Jesus' needs. They travelled down with Jesus from the north to Jerusalem for the Passover, and so were present at his crucifixion.

Jesus' total inclusion of women is illustrated by the fact that women were the first witnesses of the resurrection. After Jesus' death, the group of women followed to see where the body was laid. Then they prepared spices and perfumes, and on the first day of the week returned to anoint the body. They were the first to discover the empty tomb and to hear the news of the resurrection.[4] This is astonishing. According to first-century Judaism, a woman could not act as a witness in a court of law because it was assumed that her evidence was unreliable.[5] Yet women were chosen as the first witnesses to the resurrection, and were told to take the news of the risen Lord to the other disciples. Along with the other arguments for the historicity of the resurrection, the report about the women points to the reliability of the gospel accounts. It would have been quite outside the mindset of a first-century man to invent a story in which women were first on the scene. Such a story would have been beyond his wildest imaginings.

According to the gospels, the male disciples 'did not believe the women, because their words seemed to them like nonsense' (Lk. 24:11). Mark records that Jesus rebuked the Eleven for 'their lack of faith and their stubborn refusal to believe those who had seen him after he had risen' (Mk. 16:14).

That women were last at the cross and first at the tomb says something about their devotion to their Saviour, but it also says something about his view of them. He did not see them as a fringe following, but included them in the central events of his ministry.

Women in dialogue

The Samaritan woman

The most casual reading of the gospels reveals that on many occasions Jesus engaged in dialogue with individual women. Several of these one-to-one conversations are recorded in detail. One of the longest is the conversation with the Samaritan woman who came to draw water at Jacob's well while Jesus was resting there alone (Jn. 4:1–42).

This encounter demonstrates the extent to which Jesus was prepared to break with first-century conventions to share the good news of the gospel with a woman. In keeping with the old rabbinic proverb, 'Talk not much with womankind',[6] rabbis did not talk to women in public places.[7] Instead of avoiding her, however, Jesus deliberately opened up the conversation by asking, 'Will you give me a drink?' What makes this all the more astonishing is that she was a Samaritan, and a woman of ill repute. In the eyes of a Jewish rabbi she was sexually, racially and morally unclean. The Samaritan woman was amazed by Jesus' request; she replied, 'You are a Jew and I am a Samaritan woman. How can you ask me for a drink?' The disciples, as typical first-century men, were also surprised when they returned from the town where they had been buying food to discover that Jesus had been talking with a woman.

The conversation by the well turned into a deep theological discussion. From what follows, it is obvious that Jesus revealed himself as plainly to this woman as he did to any man. He was never disparaging, and treated her questions seriously. Jesus seemed to know all about the woman's private life. She began to realize that this stranger was someone extraordinary when he said, 'Whoever drinks the water I give him will never thirst. Indeed, the water I give him will become in him a spring of water welling up to eternal life.' They talked about the religious differences between the Jews and Samaritans, and where and how God should be worshipped. Jesus explained that 'God is spirit, and his worshippers must worship in spirit and in truth.' The discussion culminated in the woman saying, 'I know that Messiah is coming. When he comes, he will explain everything to us.' In response, Jesus declared, 'I who speak to you am he.' Leaving her water jar, the woman returned to town with the news, 'Come, see a man who told me everything I ever did. Could this be the Christ?' As a result of her testimony many other Samaritans believed that Jesus was the Saviour of the world.

The Canaanite woman

The dialogue with the Samaritan woman is not an isolated event. On another occasion, near Tyre and Sidon, another non-Jewess, a Canaanite woman, spoke to Jesus despite the disapproval of the disciples who wanted to send her away.

> A Canaanite woman from that vicinity came to him, crying out, 'Lord, Son of David, have mercy on me! My daughter is suffering terribly from demon-possession.'
>
> Jesus did not answer a word. So his disciples came to him and urged him, 'Send her away, for

she keeps crying out after us.'

He answered, 'I was sent only to the lost sheep of Israel.'

The woman came and knelt before him. 'Lord, help me!' she said.

He replied, 'It is not right to take the children's bread and toss it to their dogs.'

'Yes, Lord,' she said, 'but even the dogs eat the crumbs that fall from their masters' table.'

Then Jesus answered, 'Woman, you have great faith! Your request is granted.' (Mt. 15:21–28)

Jesus' initial response sounds harsh. However, its main purpose seems to have been to test the woman's under-standing and faith. The exchange that followed between Jesus and the woman was short, but it demonstrated that he was ready to respond to a bold woman of faith. The Canaanite woman's persuasive bargaining is reminiscent of the centurion who came to Jesus to ask help for his servant who was ill. The centurion said, 'But say the word, and my servant will be healed. For I myself am a man under authority, with soldiers under me. I tell this one, "Go", and he goes; and that one, "Come", and he comes. I say to my servant, "Do this", and he does it' (Lk. 7:7–8), The Canaanite woman and the centurion are among the few commended in the gospels for their faith.

Mary of Bethany

One incident which emphasizes the positive way in which Jesus included women is recorded in Luke 10:38–42.

As Jesus and his disciples were on their way, he came to a village where a woman named Martha opened her home to him. She had a sister called Mary, who sat at the Lord's feet listening to what he said. But Martha was distracted by all the prep-arations that had to be made. She came to him and asked, 'Lord, don't you care that my sister has left me to do the work by myself? Tell her to help me!'

We might expect Jesus to have responded by saying, 'Mary, go and give your sister a hand.' Instead, he defended Mary's right to enjoy his teaching. He replied, 'Martha, Martha . . . you are worried and upset about many things, but only one thing is needed. Mary has chosen what is better, and it will not be taken away from her.'

Jesus' response in mediating between the sisters is surprising. The church has found it difficult to assimilate this radical attitude to women. When this story is retold in sermons, more often than not it is to make the observation that some women are like Mary, but the majority are Marthas. This completely misses the point. Jesus credited Mary with having 'chosen what is better', while he cautioned Martha about her preoccupation with her domestic role. By sitting at Jesus' feet, Mary was adopting what was, in the first century, the traditional male role of a student sitting at the feet of a rabbi.[8] In the case of the Christian gospel, there was no closed circle of men around Jesus.

Jesus' attitude contrasts with the sentiments of the rabbis. In the Talmud, Rabbi Eliezer declared, 'There is no wisdom in a woman except with the distaff.' One version adds, 'It is better that the words of the Law should be burned, than that they should be given to a woman.'[9] In the Mishnah the same rabbi made a similarly strong statement when he said 'If a man gives his daughter a knowledge of the Law it is as though he taught her lechery.'[10] Jesus broke with rabbinical tradition when he taught women and included them among his followers.

Martha

A longer conversation with Martha is recorded in John 11:17–27. It took place four days after the death of her brother Lazarus. Shocked by the death of Lazarus, Martha went to meet Jesus. Her reaction might well have been, 'Why didn't you come sooner? Didn't you get our message? Why did you let him die?' Instead she said, 'Lord, if you had been here, my brother would not have died. But I know that even now God will give you whatever you ask.' Jesus did not tell her that everything was going to be all right and that he would raise Lazarus, but he carefully explained that he had power over death. In the face of bereavement Jesus pointed Martha to the only possible source of comfort when he said, 'I am the resurrection and the life. He who believes in me will live, even though he dies; and whoever lives and believes in me will never die.' Martha believed him, and in response made an impassioned declaration of faith by saying, 'I believe that you are the Christ, the Son of God, who was to come into the world.' This is one of the clearest confessions of faith in the gospels, spoken by a woman.

In the face of the awful abnormality of death Jesus suffered deep anguish. He wept for his dead friend. The conversation with Martha was a prelude to the events at the tomb. When Martha objected to the moving of the stone from the mouth of the grave, Jesus reminded her of his previous words. And having claimed to have power over death, he demonstrated it by raising Lazarus. Throughout this episode Jesus was concerned that Martha and the others present 'should believe' and see 'the glory of God'. Again, this encounter highlights the fact that there was no spiritual sexism in Jesus' treatment of women. Martha received one of the most important revelations in the gospels, and in response made one of the clearest confessions.

Women underfoot

The gospels mention four occasions on which women either washed Jesus' feet or anointed him. Those recorded in Matthew 26:6–13, Mark 14:3–9 and John 12:1–8 probably all refer to the anointing by Mary of Bethany just before the Passover, whereas Luke describes a different incident. The episode is Luke in striking.

> Now one of the Pharisees invited Jesus to have dinner with him, so he went to the Pharisee's house and reclined at the table. When a woman who had lived a sinful life in that town learned that Jesus was eating at the Pharisee's house, she brought an alabaster jar of perfume, and as she stood behind him at his feet weeping, she began to wet his feet with her tears. Then she wiped them with her hair, kissed them and poured perfume on them.
>
> When the Pharisee who had invited him saw this, he said to himself, 'If this man were a prophet, he would know who is touching him and what kind of woman she is – that she is a sinner.' (Lk. 7:36–50)

It is easy to miss the drama of this event. Let us translate it into modern terms. Imagine a smart dinner party; important religious dignitaries and scholarly theologians are present, as well as a rather unusual guest, a religious leader who has been publicly criticizing the church hierarchy and their formal pompous religion. A notorious woman has gatecrashed the party. She throws herself sobbing profusely at the guest's feet. The atmosphere becomes strained and disapproving. The analogy is not exact but we see something of the impact created by this woman. The onlookers were scandalized by her behaviour and by Jesus' response. Many contemporary women are also scandalized, though for different reasons, for they interpret this account to mean that Jesus relegated the woman to a servile position. Both first-century and twentieth-century onlookers have misinterpreted the footwashing. Jesus interprets the encounter for us.

> Jesus answered him, 'Simon, I have something to tell you.'

'Tell me, teacher,' he said.

'Two men owed money to a certain money-lender. One owed him five hundred denarii, and the other fifty. Neither of them had the money to pay him back, so he cancelled the debts of both. Now which of them will love him more?'

Simon replied, 'I suppose the one who had the bigger debt cancelled.'

'You have judged correctly,' Jesus said.

Then he turned towards the woman and said to Simon, 'Do you see this woman? I came into your house. You did not give me any water for my feet, but she wet my feet with her tears and wiped them with her hair. You did not give me a kiss, but this woman, from the time I entered, has not stopped kissing my feet. You did not put oil on my head, but she has poured perfume on my feet. Therefore, I tell you, her many sins have been forgiven – for she loved much. But he who has been forgiven little loves little.'

Then Jesus said to her, 'Your sins are forgiven.'

The other guests began to say among themselves, 'Who is this who even forgives sins?'

Jesus said to the woman, 'Your faith has saved you; go in peace.' (Lk. 7:40–50)

The footwashing was a natural expression of the woman's love and faith. Her reaction was similar to that of several other people in the gospels, who, on realizing the identity of Jesus, fell before him to worship and beg forgiveness. Simon Peter, for example, when he first recognized Jesus as God after the miraculous catch of fish, fell at Jesus' knees and said, 'Go away from me, Lord; I am a sinful man' (Lk. 5:8). Observers were always shocked when they saw Jesus receiving worship as God and offering forgiveness of sins.

The anointing of Jesus by Mary at Bethany, just before the Passover, is quite different. When the disciples objected to Mary squandering such expensive perfume, Jesus defended her, and again explained the meaning of the anointing.

'She has done a beautiful thing to me. The poor you will always have with you, but you will not always have me. When she poured this perfume on my body, she did it to prepare me for burial. I tell you the truth, wherever this gospel is preached throughout the world, what she has done will also be told, in memory of her.' (Mt. 26:10–13)

Mary's anointing was an extravagant act of worship and a prophetic gesture. She offered the precious perfume she had saved to prepare Jesus for burial.

On the subject of footwashing, it is worth noticing that on the evening before his crucifixion, Jesus himself washed the disciples' feet. During the meal, according to Luke, the disciples had been arguing about which of them was the greatest (Lk. 22:24). Jesus got up from the meal, wrapped a towel around his waist, and, taking the role of a servant, washed their feet. When he had finished, he explained what he had done:

'You call me "Teacher" and "Lord", and rightly so, for that is what I am. Now that I, your Lord and Teacher, have washed your feet, you also should wash one another's feet. I have set you an example that you should do as I have done for you. I tell you the truth, no servant is greater than his master, nor is a messenger greater than the one who sent him.' (Jn. 13:13–16)

The key to the Christian lifestyle is self-giving. Footwashing is to be the model for *both male and female* followers of Jesus.

Women made whole

Jesus showed compassion to women as well as to men in his healing ministry. For example, he healed Peter's mother-in-law (Mt. 8:14–15) and the daughter of the Canaanite woman (Mt. 15:21–28), and he raised Jairus' daughter from the dead (Lk. 8:41–56). Two of the miracles connected with women are particularly interesting and deepen our understanding of Jesus' view of women.

Mark records the episode in which the woman with the haemorrhage came up behind Jesus in the crowd, touched his cloak and was healed. According to the Levitical law this woman was ritually unclean (Lv. 15:19–30), and her touch made Jesus ceremonially unclean. But Jesus did not treat her touch as defiling; he made no attempt to cleanse himself and he did not command her to offer the sacrifice required in Leviticus. Clearly the ceremonial law is fulfilled in Jesus and no longer applies. Any apparent discrimination against women before the law in the Old Testament thus comes to an end with Jesus.

In the second incident, this time recorded by Luke, Jesus healed a crippled woman on the Sabbath (Lk. 13:10–17). The synagogue ruler was indignant because Jesus had healed on the Sabbath. But Jesus replied, 'You hypocrites! Doesn't each of you on the Sabbath untie his ox or donkey from the stall and lead it out to give it water? Then should not this woman, a daughter of Abraham, whom Satan has kept bound for eighteen long years, be set free on the Sabbath day from what has bound her?' Significantly, Jesus called the woman 'a daughter of Abraham'. In other words, she was a full member of the religious community and a recipient of the promise given to Abraham. This incident stands in sharp contrast to an occasion that John records, when Jesus questioned whether a group of disbelieving Jews were true descendants of Abraham (Jn. 8:31–41). Jesus judges people by their response to him and his teaching, not by whether they are male or female.

Women outsiders

Many of the religious leaders found Jesus' acceptance of the disreputable and marginal in society very offensive. A number of women outsiders – the Samaritan woman, the Canaanite woman, the immoral and the ceremonially unclean, for example – were among those who flocked to him. John recalls another woman outsider who was used as a test case to ensnare Jesus.

Jesus was teaching in the temple courts, with all the people gathered around him, when the teachers of the law and the Pharisees brought in a woman caught in adultery. They made her stand before the group and said to Jesus, 'Teacher, this woman was caught in the act of adultery. In the Law Moses commanded us to stone such women. Now what do you say?' They omitted to say that the law of Moses also commanded that the man found sleeping with the woman was to be put to death (Dt. 22:22–24).

Jesus replied, 'If any one of you is without sin, let him be the first to throw a stone at her.' As he stooped down and wrote on the ground the woman's accusers melted away until Jesus and the woman were left alone. Then Jesus asked her, 'Woman, where are they? Has no-one condemned you?' 'No-one, sir,' she said. 'Then neither do I condemn you,' Jesus declared. 'Go now and leave your life of sin' (Jn. 8:2–11).

Rembrandt's painting of the woman taken in adultery captures the essence of what took place in this encounter. The religious leaders ranged around Jesus are depicted in dark colours, pointing the finger at the fallen woman. In contrast, the woman in the foreground wears white. Jesus' words have turned the woman's accusers into the accused. The men fall into their own trap. Jesus exposes their hypocrisy. Unlike the hypocrites who dragged her into the temple courts, the woman goes away forgiven.

Subject women

Jesus did not make pronouncements about a woman's nature or a woman's place. Nor did he illustrate his teaching exclusively from male experience. In fact sometimes he appears deliberately to pair incidents from men's and women's lives to make a point (*e.g.* Lk. 15:3–10), providing the perfect pattern for the use of inclusive illustrations and language in teaching. He never used women as negative examples, as was so common in rabbinical teaching. He referred to women positively and used illustrations from their everyday lives to teach spiritual truths.

A widow repeatedly presenting her case before a judge is a powerful reminder of the need for persistence in prayer (Lk. 18:1–8); a woman adding yeast to flour to make dough depicts the hidden growth of God's kingdom (Mt. 13:33); and a woman rejoicing over the discovery of her lost silver coin is used to explain the rejoicing in heaven over one sinner who repents (Lk. 15:8–10). The patient bridesmaids are examples of how to wait for the return of Jesus (Mt. 25:1–13), and the moving story of the widow and her mite illustrates that God assesses gifts not by their size but by the commitment on the part of the giver (Mk. 12:41–44). Jesus' teaching also recalls earlier women, like the widow who sheltered Elijah, who were of little importance in the eyes of society but significant in God's eyes (Lk. 4:25–27).

In the sermon on the mount Jesus came down hard on the way women are reduced to sexual objects. In the context of teaching that thoughts are as important as actions he said: 'You have heard that it was said, "Do not commit adultery." But I tell you that anyone who looks at a woman lustfully has already committed adultery with her in his heart' (Mt. 5:27–28).

Mary Evans regards this statement as perhaps the key to understanding Jesus' attitude to women.

Jesus, in contrast to the rabbis, completely dismisses

the suggestion that lust is inevitable. He does not warn his followers against looking at a woman, but against doing so with lust. Women are to be recognised as subjects in their own right, as fellow human beings, fellow disciples, and not just the objects of men's desire.[11]

Unlike the rabbis, therefore, Jesus did not teach his disciples to avoid the opposite sex, and he never taught the separation or seclusion of women. This explains why women were free to join in his ministry.

Jesus' teaching on marriage and divorce was also original, and must have sounded most unusual to his first-century hearers. In contrast to the rabbis, who allowed only the husband to initiate divorce, Jesus put both partners on the same footing (Mk. 10:1–12). He also made it clear that the only acceptable reason for divorce is marital unfaithfulness (Mt. 19:3–8).

Jesus never stereotyped women. A woman's value is not determined by her domestic, maternal or sexual functions, but by her relationship to God. On one occasion as Jesus was going through a crowd a woman shouted out, 'Blessed is the mother who gave you birth and nursed you.' Jesus replied, 'Blessed rather are those who hear the word of God and obey it' (Lk. 11:27–28). Jesus refused to sentimentalize motherhood. The most important fact about any woman is her response to the gospel.

The gospel is for both sexes. Jesus addressed both men and women in his public ministry. The inclusion is very clear. He declared, 'Whoever does the will of my Father in heaven is my brother and sister and mother' (Mt. 12:50). The cost, responsibilities and consequences of discipleship are the same for both men and women (Mt. 10:34–39). Jesus made no distinctions between men and women; both are guilty before God and need to repent and be forgiven.

Women in revolution

How revolutionary, then, was Jesus' view of women? Theologians differ in their responses to this question. His conduct and teaching are usually compared with the mores of first-century Judaism. But the Talmud and the Mishnah, which are the main sources of information about Judaism during this period, date from between the second and the sixth centuries AD. They present a very oppressive view of women. Some argue that the situation may have been freer in gospel times. But some of the Mishnaic and Talmudic attitudes to women can be cross-checked by comparing them with earlier materials.[12]

As always there are several ways of interpreting the facts. At one extreme, there are those who overstate the revolution in women's roles and make exaggerated claims about the leadership roles of Jesus' female followers. At the other extreme are those who understate the revolution, minimize the involvement of women in Jesus' ministry, and lay the emphasis very firmly on the twelve apostles as inaugurating all-male church leadership. Both groups impose on the text a twentieth-century preoccupation with ordination, official titles and ecclesiastical hierarchies. The gospels are remarkably silent on these issues. We must look elsewhere in the New Testament for teaching on the leadership structure of the early church.

There seems to be general agreement that the way Jesus spoke to women in public, taught them, allowed them to follow him and actively participate in his ministry represented a radical break with rabbinic Judaism and, at certain points, with the Old Testament. Under the Mosaic law, especially as interpreted by the rabbis in the intertestamental period, only the free, Jewish male was a full member of the religious community. Women, slaves and Gentiles did not share the same religious privileges. They were separated from the men in the synagogues and were kept out of the holiest parts of the temple; they were not required to study the law and were not counted as part of the assembly. In Christ, believers share the same spiritual status regardless of sex, race and class. Paul spelt this out in the letter to the church in Galatia when he wrote, 'There is neither Jew nor Greek, slave nor free, male nor female, for you are all one in Christ Jesus' (Gal. 3:28).

The disciples, as typical first-century men, provide an indication of the extent to which Jesus' treatment of women was a departure from the norm. On several occasions, they found it difficult to understand Jesus' attitudes. Not only were they surprised to discover him talking alone with the Samaritan woman (Jn. 4:4–26), but they were indignant when a woman anointed him with costly perfume (Mt. 26:6–13), and actively discouraged women and children from coming to Jesus (Mt. 15:21–28; 19:13–14). The religious leaders, too, took exception to Jesus allowing a woman to anoint him (Lk. 7:36–39), healing a woman on the Sabbath (Lk. 13:15–16) and forgiving an adulteress (Jn. 8:2–11). In fact, Marcion claimed that Jesus' association with women was one of the charges brought against him at his trial.[13]

Jesus's attitudes run counter to those of any culture. He valued women, affirming them as being equally made in the image of God and fully human. There is no hint of oppression, domination, depreciation or ridicule in his interactions with women. He never silenced or interrupted them, nor did he ever appear to be threatened by them. His words and actions clearly convey that women count just as much as men. No man before or since has behaved as he did. I often think that only God could have been so completely free of sexism.

But did the early church follow Jesus' example? Some would argue that the apostle Paul, the subject of the next chapter, soon undid Jesus' good work and introduced savage anti-feminism into the church.

Notes

1 J. Jeremias, *New Testament Theology* (SCM, 1971), p. 376.

2 Why did Jesus choose twelve male disciples? He tells us that the number twelve represents the tribes of Israel (Lk. 22:30), but he does not tell us why they were all men. Some branches of the church believe that Jesus' choice of the Twelve inaugurates an all-male apostolic succession. Some of the bishops and elders in the early church may indeed have been appointed by missionary apostles, but the evidence is not conclusive. There are few facts to support the case that sacramental powers were passed on by direct lineal contact with the apostles. See E. M. Howe, *Women and Church Leadership* (Zondervan, 1982), pp. 70–3.

Biblical feminists, on the other hand, often argue that women were exluded from the Twelve because it would have been culturally unacceptable for women to be the constant companions of Jesus and the leaders of the early church. They point out that there were probably no Gentiles and no slaves among the apostles. Did Jesus therefore, intend to establish sex, race and class as criteria for church office? (See M. Evans, *Woman in the Bible*, Paternoster, 1983, pp. 49–51.) The gospels are completely silent on this question. We must look elsewhere in the New Testament to find the qualifications for church leaders.

3 Mt. 27:55–56; Mk. 15:40.

4 Mt. 28:1–10; Mk. 15:47 – 16:11; Lk. 23:55 – 24:11; Jn. 20:1–18.

5 On the social position of women see Jeremias, *New Testament Theology*, p. 374.

6 Proverb of Jose b. Johanan of Jerusalem, *c*.150 BC, quoted in Jeremias, *New Testament Theology*, p. 360.

7 Some evidence indicates that there was stricter separation of women among the wealthier urban classes, but 'it was not customary even in the country for a man to converse with a strange woman', Jeremias, *New Testament Theology*, pp. 362–3.

8 'To sit at the feet of' may be a technical formula. Paul, for example, described himself as sitting at the feet of Gamaliel (Acts 22:3).

9 Quoted in J. B. Hurley, *Man and Woman in Biblical Perspective* (IVP, 1981), p. 72.

10 Quoted in Hurley, *Man and Woman*, p. 73.

11 Evans, *Woman in the Bible*, p. 45.

12 On the Talmud and Mishnah see Hurley, *Man and Woman*, p. 58.

13 On Marcion see Evans, *Woman in the Bible*, p. 47, and Jeremias, *New Testament Theology*, p. 226.

CHAPTER EIGHT

Competing interpretations of Paul

At every step of the way, feminists had to fight the conception that they were violating the God-given nature of woman. Clergymen interrupted women's rights conventions, waving Bibles and quoting from the Scriptures: 'Saint Paul said: . . . "and the head of every woman is man" . . . "Let your women be silent in the churches, for it is not permitted unto them to speak" . . . "And if they will learn anything, let them ask their husbands at home; for it is a shame for women to speak in the church" . . . "But I suffer not a woman to teach, nor usurp authority over the man, but to be in silence; for Adam was first formed, then Eve." '[1]

IN describing the history of the women's movement in the United States, Betty Friedan caricatures the apostle Paul. At the same time, she captures in essence the traditional interpretation of his teaching. This interpretation has tended to lift the apostle's statements about silence and submission out of context and to emphasize these texts at the expense of other New Testament passages. Woman becomes the submissive, second sex. The idea of woman's subjection is confirmed by referring to the interpretation of Genesis which sees woman as inferior, the afterthought of God and not quite in the divine image. Woman's sinfulness at the fall must be punished through submission.

In reaction to this interpretation, some biblical feminists have majored on the text, 'There is neither Jew nor Greek, slave nor free, male nor female, for you are all one in Christ Jesus' (Gal. 3:28). For them this is the great breakthrough, the Magna Carta of Christian liberty.[2] Sexual equality becomes the hermeneutical key by which the Scriptures must be interpreted. This often means that Paul's apparently repressive, rabbinical teaching is rejected in favour of his more enlightened teaching on the equality of the sexes. Some would claim that there is a double current in Paul's thinking; that he was torn between his new-found Christianity and his old rabbinic training.[3] It becomes the task of biblical interpreters to sift the texts to unearth Paul's Christian teaching.

The traditional interpretation of Paul argues for woman's subordination, the biblical feminist interpretation for the equality of the sexes. These Pauline texts have taken on enormous ideological significance. A great deal is at stake in the interpretation of a few difficult passages. Confronted with the diversity in Paul's teaching, the response of both anti-feminists and feminists has been to read Paul's letters selectively. Beginning with the axiom either that woman is subordinate or that the sexes are equal, each group has found evidence to support its view. While paying lip-service to the principle of harmonizing Scripture, interpreters have tended to play the 'mirror game'.[4] The traditional interpretation 'makes Genesis 1 – 2 mirror what 1 Corinthians 11 mixed with Ephesians 5:21–33 says. And then 1 Corinthians 11 is made to say exactly what Genesis 2 has been made to say.'[5] Other texts which do not fit neatly into the traditional interpretation are minimized and Paul's inclusion of women in his ministry is ignored.

In search of the real Paul

Why are there so many interpretations of Paul's letters? Is the apostle's teaching so confused and contradictory? I do not believe that it is, though *we* may be confused in expecting to discover dogmatic answers to questions which were not asked in the New Testament. Paul did not share the same ideological concerns as his twentieth-century readers. The parts of Paul's letters which deal with women are notoriously difficult to interpret. They are among the most difficult passages in the New Testament. There are two main factors which contribute to these difficulties.

First, we cannot always identify the historical context into which Paul was writing. He wrote to address problems in the churches; without knowing the local situations it is difficult for us to understand his responses. We cannot always be certain whether Paul's teaching applies only to that particular local church situation or whether it is to be applied universally. In 1 Timothy 2, for example, Paul may be writing about false teaching and heresy in the church at Ephesus or he may be enunciating principles that are normative for every church situation. 1 Corinthians 11:3–15 describes a practice which may refer to a veiling or to the way the women wore their hair.[6] We cannot imitate the Corinthian women because we do not know exactly what they were doing. Perhaps what the apostle Paul was most concerned about was that the women were flaunting customs which distinguished between the sexes and making Christianity appear like the cults.[7] Today, we have to find appropriate contemporary cultural modes of affirming sexual differentiation.

Secondly, the passages about women are full of ambiguous expressions and sometimes contain words which are difficult to translate. In 1 Corinthians 11:10 Paul writes, 'For this reason, and because of the angels, the woman ought to have a sign of authority on her head.' What does this mean? Why does he mention the angels? Is he referring to the role of the angels in worship? In 1 Corinthians 14:34 he writes, 'Women should remain silent in the churches. They are not allowed to speak, but must be in submission, as the Law says.' Which law? Is he referring to a rabbinic tradition, or to the Old Testament, or to Genesis 3:16? We cannot be certain. In 1 Timothy 2:15 Paul says, 'But women will be saved through childbirth – if they continue in faith, love and holiness with propriety.' This sounds as if godly women are spared the pain of childbirth. But this obviously is not the case. Many a God-fearing woman has died in childbirth. So what did Paul mean? He cannot have meant that women are saved by their good works; that would contradict the rest of Scripture. It may be an obscure allusion to the messianic promise in Genesis 3:15 that the one who would crush the serpent's head would be born of a woman, or it could be a response to heretical teaching which devalued childbirth and marriage.

In 1 Timothy 2:12 Paul writes, 'I do not permit a woman to teach or to have authority over a man; she must be silent.' This verse presents several problems to the translator. Paul uses the word *authentein*, rather than the more common word *exousiazein*, for 'have authority'. The word is crucial in understanding Paul's command. But this is the only time that *authentein* is used in the New Testament. There are few known uses of the word. It appears to be a strong word and may mean 'usurp authority', 'domineer', 'initiate', 'claim authorship' or 'wrongfully use authority'. It may have sexual overtones. In his commentary, John Chrysostom (d. 407) understood 1 Timothy as speaking about sexual licence. Were the women who were influenced by the fertility cults teaching immorality? Clement of Alexandria (d. *c.* 215), in his complaint about those who turn love feasts into orgies, used the word *authentes*.[8] It is also possible to translate the first part of Paul's sentence, 'I am not at present permitting . . . '[9] which dramatically alters his command into a temporary injunction which applied only to the situation in Ephesus. Another problem for translators is that Greek uses the word *gynē* for both 'woman' and 'wife', and *anēr* for both 'man' and 'husband'. In 1 Corinthians 14 and 1 Timothy 2 we cannot be certain if Paul was addressing his comments to wives or more generally to women.

I do not know how many times I have heard the *cri de coeur*, 'It is so important; why isn't it clearer? Why didn't Paul make it clearer?' How many of us would love to sit down with the apostle and ask, 'Paul, what exactly did you mean?'

I suspect that it is not clearer because it was not that important in the early church. Part of the problem is that we look at the New Testament through twentieth-century spectacles. I am not sure that the first-century church shared our preoccupation with ecclesiastical structures and status. Maybe they were too busy spreading the gospel to be concerned about precise job descriptions for women in their churches.

What Paul did not say

Like Jesus, Paul never made pronouncements about woman's nature. Most of his teaching was not sex-specific and was directed at both male and female believers. Interestingly, he told all believers that 'the fruit of the Spirit is love, joy, peace, patience, kindness, goodness, faithfulness, gentleness and self-control', and commanded women as well as men to 'be strong in the Lord'.[10] There is no feminine mystique according to Paul.

From the day of Pentecost, it is clear that women as well as men receive the Holy Spirit, just as Joel had prophesied.

'In the last days, God says,
I will pour out my Spirit on all people.
Your sons and daughters will prophesy,
    your young men will see visions,
    your old men will dream dreams.
Even on my servants, both men and women,

159

I will pour out my Spirit in those days,
and they will prophesy.' (Acts 2:17–18)

Pentecost sanctions women prophesying. Spiritual gifts are given to both sexes. Paul wrote to the church in Corinth, 'Now to each one the manifestation of the Spirit is given for the common good' (1 Cor. 12:7). He never suggested that women are excluded from the work of the Holy Spirit.

Hardly surprisingly, women were as visible in Paul's ministry as they were in that of Jesus. Lydia, the seller of purple cloth, was the first to respond to Paul's message in Philippi, and the church which Paul founded may have begun meeting in her home (Acts 16:13–15). Two other women in Philippi, Euodia and Syntyche, are described as 'women who have contended at my side in the cause of the gospel' (Phil. 4:3). 'Not a few prominent women' became Christians in Thessalonica (Acts 17:4) and Damaris is named among the converts in Athens (Acts 17:34). Part of the church in Colosse met in the house of Nympha (Col. 4:15). Phoebe was a *diakonos* or deacon of the church in Cenchrea, and a *prostatis*, 'protectress', 'helper', 'legal representative' or 'one who stands before many' (Rom. 16:1–2).[11] Priscilla and her husband Aquila are called 'fellow-workers in Christ Jesus'[12] for their work in the Gentile churches in Corinth, Ephesus and Rome.[13] They had risked their lives to protect Paul. Mary, Tryphena, Tryphosa and Persis in Rome are described as having worked hard or as being workers in the Lord (Rom. 16:6, 12). Several other unnamed women travelled with their husbands on missionary journeys (1 Cor. 9:5). Men and women faced danger, discomfort and death in the cause of the gospel. They were exciting times as the church spread from the Eastern Mediterranean into the rest of the known world, and the picture that emerges is of women involved alongside the men. Whatever Paul *was* saying, then, he was *not* saying that women could play no active part in the expansion of the church.

Neither male nor female

In his letter to the church in Galatia, Paul explained the rationale for including women as full members of the religious community. He wrote: 'There is neither Jew nor Greek, slave nor free, male nor female, for you are all one in Christ Jesus' (Gal. 3:28).

It is important to understand the context in which Paul made this statement. The main purpose of his letter was to refute the teaching of the circumcision party who were insisting that Gentile believers should be circumcised. Paul argued vigorously that a person is not justified by observance of the law but by faith in Christ (Gal. 2:15–21).

In this context he showed that the religious distinctions of the Old Testament no longer applied. In the Old Testament only the free male Jew was a full member of the religious community. This was no longer true. Gentiles, slaves and women, if they belonged to Christ, were also included. Racial, social and sexual distinctions are irrelevant in our relationship with God. The gospel cuts through the major divisions in society. Paul's statement in Galatians 3:28 is extraordinary for an ex-rabbi; it is very radical. The sexes are equal in salvation. Women have the same spiritual status before God as men. They are one in Christ. Discrimination is replaced by unity. Woman's new status in Christ has social consequences. Peter reminded husbands to be considerate to their wives; the reason he gave is that wives are 'heirs with you of the gracious gift of life' (1 Pet. 3:7). They are joint heirs.

Traditional interpretations have sometimes overlooked Paul's statement in Galatians. Other Pauline letters have been interpreted to mean that there are differences in the way men and women relate to God. This is particularly true of headship. Paul's comments about the husband being head of the wife have been taken to mean that the man stands between his wife and God; he is her covering.[14] Man becomes a superior intermediary between God and woman. But such teaching runs counter to Galatians 3:28 and to New Testament teaching about the priesthood of all believers (1 Pet. 2:5, 9).

On the other hand, some theologians may use the text in Galatians to relativize the differences between men and women and minimize biblical teaching about the complementarity of the sexes.[15] Galatians teaches that men and women have the same relationship to God, not that men and women are exactly the same. This text is not an argument for adrogyny. It is discrimination under Jewish law that is removed, not all created sexual distinctions. Unity does not mean uniformity.

Heads you win, submit you lose

I once read a review of a book on cohabitation contracts. I was struck by the emphasis in all the sample contracts on the rights of the individual: rights to property, rights to children, rights to child support and rights to a career. The same emphasis on rights may be apparent among interpreters of Paul's teaching on marriage. At one extreme are those who argue for a hierarchical model to establish the husband's right to rule and to emphasize the differences between the sexes. At the other are those who argue for an egalitarian model to give equal rights to husband and wife and to relativize the differences between the sexes. Both models fall short of the biblical ideal as set out by Paul in Ephesians 5. He made no mention of rights, only of the obligations of husband and wife. His model marriage is one of self-giving in which each partner loves the other unconditionally. It is a picture of unity and diversity.

Instead of emphasizing rights, Paul described the responsibilities of both partners. These are revolutionary by the standards of any culture. He began by telling husband and wife to 'submit to one another out of reverence for Christ' (Eph. 5:21), then went on to set an extraordinary standard of self-giving for them both. It is a tragedy that

Ephesians 5 has been understood as endorsing an oppressive model of marriage; it does just the opposite. The events
described in Genesis 3 marked the beginning of hostilities
between the sexes. The teaching of Ephesians 5, by putting
the emphasis on self-giving, is designed to avoid the power
struggle that was set in motion in Eden.

Paul explained the husband's headship by giving two
illustrations. Husbands are to love their wives 'just as
Christ loved the church and gave himself up for her' (Eph.
5:25) and 'as their own bodies' (Eph. 5:28). Headship is
primarily defined in terms of self-giving. Headship is not
tyranny. John Chrysostom commented:

> Take then the same provident care for her, as Christ
> takes for the church. Yes, even if it shall be needful
> for you to give your life for her, yes, and to be cut
> into ten thousand pieces, yes, and to endure and
> undergo any suffering whatever, refuse it not.
> Though you should undergo all this, yet you will
> not, no, not even then, have done anything like
> Christ.[16]

In his first letter to the church in Corinth, Paul compared
the relationship between the sexes to the relationship
between God and Christ. He wrote: 'Now I want you to
realize that the head of every man is Christ, and the head
of the woman is man, and head of Christ is God' (1 Cor.
11:3). The relationship between man and woman reflects
the unity and diversity of the Trinity. This is a beautiful
picture. The Father and Son are equal but the Father is
head. It would never occur to us to think that because God
is described as the head of Christ, Christ is exploited in
this relationship. So we should not assume that man's being
head of the woman means exploitation. 'Man's headship
of the woman is no more incompatible with the equality of
the sexes than the Father's headship of the Son is incompatible with the unity of the Godhead.'[17]

In the same passage in 1 Corinthians 11, Paul based

headship on creation reminding us that woman was created 'from' and 'for' the man. This has often been understood as a savage, anti-feminist statement, but this is to misunderstand Paul's meaning. He was very careful to qualify his remarks on Genesis 2 by adding, 'In the Lord, however, woman is not independent of man, nor is man independent of woman. For as woman came from man, so also man is born of woman. But everything comes from God' (1 Cor. 11:12). Man is not superior to, or closer to God than, woman.

To summarize the argument: in Ephesians 5 headship is primarily defined as self-giving and sacrifice. A man is to love his wife as Christ loved the church and as his own body. In 1 Corinthians 11 headship is based on creation and on the relationship between God and Christ. So far so good, but a host of questions remain. Does the husband exercise authority over the wife? What is the wife's role in decision-making? Does the husband's career come first? According to the Bible, should a woman never take initiative? What is the practical outworking of headship?

Traditional interpretations tend to equate headship with superior rank and authority, and to emphasize female subordination.[18] The marriage relationship becomes one of superior to subordinate. In this inegalitarian model of marriage, headship is easily distorted into domination. In this context, headship means little more than the casting vote when a couple reach stalemate in a disagreement.

This view has been challenged by interpreters anxious to demonstrate that the word 'head', *kephalē*, may also mean 'source' or 'origin', or the literal head or top of a person, and does not necessarily mean 'ruler'. They argue, for example, that the Septuagint translators used fourteen different words to translate the Hebrew word *rosh*, 'chief' or 'leader'. If Paul had been thinking about the husband as authority he could have used more common Greek words for authority, such as *exousia* (Rom. 13:1–2) or *archōn* (Romans 13:3).[19] They emphasize that on the occasions when Paul uses *kephalē* he often appears to have the metaphor of the interdependence of head and body in mind. This metaphor suggests the 'mutual dependence and unity' of husband and wife.[20] The debate continues to rage around Greek lexicons and the seven New Testament passages where Christ is described as the head of the church.[21] It is difficult to escape the fact that 'head' has a connotation of authority. It is obvious in the headship of Christ over the church (Eph. 1:22) that Christ has authority over the church as well as being her source, and authority is also involved in the Trinitarian relationship in which God is the head of Christ.

Whatever the precise meaning or meanings of *kephalē*, the emphasis in Ephesians 5 is that the husband is to imitate Christ not as sovereign over the church but in his loving sacrifice on her behalf. The comparison of the husband and Christ is not an exact one. Ephesians 5 does not teach the superiority or divinity of the husband. We must not push the analogy too far. It is obvious, for example, that the husband does not act as saviour for his wife.

The New Testament defines headship primarily as service. The husband is to lead in self-sacrificial service. If the husband is given authority it is to be expressed by love and care, not by domination. 'If "headship" means "power" in any sense, then it is power to care not to crush, power to serve not to dominate, power to facilitate self-fulfilment, not to frustrate or destroy it.'[22] How could a husband who is trying to put this into practice contemplate making decisions with no reference to his wife? How could a Christian husband subject his wife to violence and brutal domination? The Bible holds out a warning that if men do not live considerately with their wives, and do not treat them with respect as the weaker vessel (presumably this means the more vulnerable physically), then their prayers will be hindered (1 Pet. 3:7).

Paul does not use the word 'authority' to describe the husband's position. The only time the Greek word *exousiazein*, 'have authority', is used in the context of the marital relationship is in 1 Corinthians 7:4 where Paul talks of the wife having authority over the husband's body and the husband over the wife's. First he says, 'The wife's body does not belong to her alone but also to her husband', which we might expect a first-century man to say. But he adds, 'In the same way, the husband's body does not belong to him alone but also to his wife.' In Christian marriage it is a case of mutual ownership. This was very radical teaching for the ancient world. Reciprocity is fundamental to Christian marriage.

It would be easy for a wife to take advantage of a husband who gave himself so totally on her behalf, but Paul sets an equally high standard of self-giving for her. He explains that a wife is to submit to her husband as the church submits to Christ, and by implication as Christ submits to the Father.[23] There could hardly be more exacting guidelines for a wife's actions and attitudes. In Ephesians 5 Paul begins the command to the woman with 'but', though this is not present in all translations. Ephesians 5:24 should read, 'But as the church is subject to Christ, so let wives be subject in everything to their husbands.'[24] The implication is that she, too, must behave responsibly. The word used for 'submission' has military connotations; the wife is 'to order' herself so that she and her husband function as one.[25] The onus is on the wife to give herself voluntarily, not on the husband to make her submit.

It is obvious from elsewhere in the Bible that a wife's submission is not to be equated with mindless obedience and passivity in the face of a husband's sinfulness. In the early church Sapphira was punished for aiding Ananias in his deceit (Acts 5:1–11). Nor does submission mean subjection to domesticity. Of course the Bible talks about a married woman's responsibilities to her family; one of her priorities will be lovingly to care for her children.[26] But the husband is also told to 'manage his own family well' and to bring up children 'in the training and instruction of the Lord'.[27] The woman who is idealized in Proverbs 31:10–31 does not have a narrowly defined role; she demonstrates her competence in many different areas of life. As well as caring for the needs of her family and maintaining good relationships with her husband and children, she is also involved in a business venture (verse 16) and in aiding the poor and needy (verse 20). The whole picture suggests a strong, competent woman who is not afraid to take initiative.

Sarah is held up as an example for Christian women to emulate because she 'obeyed Abraham and called him her master' (1 Pet. 3:6). We can safely say that 'master' was a term of address that was limited to a particular cultural context. But in many ways the reference to Sarah's obedience is puzzling. Twice in the Old Testament Sarah obeyed Abraham by sinning. She pretended to be his sister and almost became entangled in adulterous relationships (Gn. 12:10–20; 20:1–18). The couple's half-truths incurred God's judgment. Clearly her obedience on these occasions was a recipe for disaster. What then are we to imitate? Perhaps what is at stake is her fundamental attitude, especially to God's command to Abraham to leave Ur; she did not frustrate God's overall purpose for their lives.

The Bible does not spell out the details of the practical outworking of these commands to husband and wife. It does not tell us how to organize the division of labour in a home, or which style of parenting to adopt, or whether dual career structures are advisable. It tells us much more about the relationship between two people. Part of the beauty of the Bible is that it recognizes the diversity of couples in different cultures and allows us freedom to work out how to put its precepts into practice. Christian marriage should be a competition in self-giving, not for rights. The husband's love and the wife's submission, though distinctive, are both expressions of mutual submission out of reverence for Christ (Eph. 5:21), which is to characterize all believers. In fact, submission and love are both aspects of the same self-forgetful self-giving. The goal is unity. In Ephesians 5, Paul echoes Genesis 2:24, 'the two will become one flesh', indicating that the pattern he outlines is the way to return to God's original, pre-fall purpose for marriage.

Seen and not heard

> In a male supremacist society where women are devalued, their language is devalued to such an extent that they are required to be silent. Within this framework it becomes 'logical' to have one rule for women's talk and another for men because it is the sex and not just the talk which is significant.[28]

Is Paul a supremacist condemning women to silence? Does the Christian church believe that women have nothing valuable to say? In many Christian gatherings men occupy the pulpits and platforms while women are passive spectators. It is customary in some church traditions for men to pray and preach and for women to listen. This may mean that immature young men are allowed to voice their opinions while mature women with years of experience in Christian living are silenced.

Is this a true reflection of the biblical pattern? Many would argue that it is. The proof-texts used in support of women's silence are 1 Corinthians 14:34 and 1 Timothy 2:11-12. On first reading, the command in 1 Corinthians 14:34 seems clear enough; in fact Paul uses very strong language: 'As in all congregations of the saints, women should remain silent in the churches. They are not allowed to speak, but must be in submission, as the Law says.'

But if we read the text in context, its meaning is not quite so obvious. Three chapters earlier, in 1 Corinthians 11:5, Paul writes about women praying and prophesying. Then in 1 Corinthians 14:34 he tells them to be silent. How are we to reconcile these two passages? Several possibilities have been suggested.

First, some maintain that in 1 Corinthians 11 Paul was permitting a less than ideal situation which he later corrected. Calvin favoured this interpretation on the grounds that when Paul 'takes them to task because they were prophesying bare-headed, he is not giving them permission, however, to prophesy in any other way whatever, but rather is delaying the censure of that fault to another passage'.[29] This is not very convincing. If Paul were convinced that it was wrong for women to pray and prophesy, why would he set out how and why they should do so?

Others hold that 1 Corinthians 11 and 1 Corinthians 14 are discussing different situations, one public and the other private. Women are commanded to silence in the public church situation.[30] This sounds plausible, but there is no evidence in the text to support this interpretation. It is doubtful whether the early church made such a distinction between formal and informal gatherings of the church.

A third view is that the women were being disorderly in some way, possibly chatting or shouting out questions, and Paul was forbidding this disorderly behaviour. This seems quite plausible, especially in the light of the verses which follow, telling women to ask questions of their husbands at home (1 Cor. 14:35). If women were separated from their husbands, as in the synagogue, they may have been shouting to them across the church. This interpretation depends on the translation of *lalein* ('speak'), which can be translated 'chatter', 'talk nonsensically', or even 'speak in tongues', though Paul is usually more specific when he refers to speaking in tongues. Catherine Kroeger suggests that the Corinthian church was influenced by the enthusiasm and disorder of the mystery cults.[31] Perhaps these women were dominating worship as happened in the cults.

Fourthly, some believe that the women were being forbidden to join in the dialogue or to teach, hence the reference to asking questions at home. If this interpretation is correct, *lalein* refers to asking questions and not to all forms of speech.[32] This interpretation is favoured by those who believe women should be excluded from all teaching roles.

A fifth possibility is that women were being forbidden to join in the judgment of prophecy which is described in the previous verses. It is assumed that women were forbidden to do this because they would be undertaking a teaching role and exercising authority.[33] Sometimes this is interpreted more specifically as a command to wives forbidding them to judge and interrupt their husbands' prophecy, thus causing conflict in public, but it is strange that Paul did not use the possessive pronoun if he had the marriage relationship in mind.[34]

Finally, some assert that the opinion expressed by Paul about women was not his own, but one which he quoted in order to repudiate it.[35] 'You only' is in the masculine form. Was he in fact very firmly rebuking men who silence women (verse 36)? He used the same method in 1 Corinthians 6:12.

It is impossible to be dogmatic about which interpretation is correct. But it is clear that 1 Corinthians 14 is not an absolute command to women to seal their lips in every situation; this would contradict Paul's teaching in 1 Corinthians 11 about women praying and prophesying. In the immediate context, too, Paul says: 'When you come together, everyone has a hymn, or a word of instruction, a revelation, a tongue or an interpretation' (1 Cor. 14:26). His comment is not sex-specific.

If the command to women to be silent is Paul's own opinion rather than one which he is quoting, it can be seen as the third in a series of commands Paul gave to help the Corinthian church worship and exercise spiritual gifts in an orderly way. In these injunctions Paul set out the conditions under which men as well as women were to be silent in the church. In each command he addressed a different group of people and told them to be silent under certain circumstances. He issued the same command three times, and it is obvious in the first two cases that the silence which is commanded is not absolute but is qualified by the context. First, he told those who speak in tongues that they are to be silent if an interpreter is not present (verses 27–28). Secondly, he told the prophets to prophesy in turn; if someone who is sitting down wants to prophesy, the first speaker should be silent. In both cases these commands are conditional and are to regulate order in worship. Thirdly, Paul addressed the women and gave them exactly the same command. This also appears to be a conditional command, though in the case of the women it is more difficult to discern the condition. Since Paul is so concerned with order in worship, and because of the strong call to submission and self-control, it seems likely that the women were being over-enthusiastic or disruptive in some way; chatting, asking questions or perhaps challenging their husbands publicly.

'I do not permit a woman to teach . . . '

It is recorded that when Lucy Stone, an abolitionist and women's rights campaigner, was born in 1818, her mother said, 'Oh dear! I am sorry it is a girl. A woman's life is so hard.' Lucy was soon to discover the truth of her mother's words. After a lengthy struggle, she was permitted to enter Oberlin College to follow a classical course, only to discover a great deal of discrimination against women students. At the end of her course it was proposed that a man should read her graduation address, since it was thought improper for a woman to read her paper in front of the men.[36]

The apostle Paul has been invoked on many similar occasions to silence women and make them marginal to the mainstream of human activity. But can we be sure that this is really what he had in mind? Part of Paul's first letter to Timothy in Ephesus (1 Tim. 2:12–15) has been made to bear enormous weight. It is a problematic passage and again there are several possible interpretations.

Traditionally, the statement 'I do not permit a woman to teach or to have authority over a man' has been interpreted as an absolute command which should be applied universally.[37] Under no circumstances, therefore, should a woman teach or exercise authority over a man. She is prohibited from taking office as a teacher, and especially from being responsible for the regular teaching of a church. Women are to learn quietly and submissively; they are not to teach authoritatively.

This interpretation is supported by the fact that Paul bases his command to women on the creation and fall narratives. He says, 'For Adam was formed first, then Eve. And Adam was not the one deceived; it was the woman who was deceived and became a sinner' (1 Tim. 2:13–14). Woman is not to teach because, it is argued, to do so would not reflect God's original purpose of female subordination. A woman who teaches and exercises authority, therefore, overturns the creation order. Why does Paul found his command on the account of the fall in Genesis 3 as well as on the creation order of Genesis 2? Some interpreters have assumed that woman is unfit to teach because she is more gullible and easily deceived; she is silenced because of her sin. But elsewhere Paul specifically commands women to teach women and children. Surely he would have forbidden this if women were generally more prone to deception (Tit. 2:3–5).

Other evidence that favours this interpretation is Paul's statement that he was writing so that 'you will know how people ought to conduct themselves in God's household' (1 Tim. 3:15). Also, the command immediately precedes the list of qualifications for elders, whose role is to teach and care for the church; it is therefore argued that Paul made it clear that women were excluded from this position before he set out the requirements. Paul seems to reinforce this by stating that an overseer is to be 'the husband of but one wife', suggesting that all overseers would be male. This is taken by some as an argument for women's exclusion from this office. Interpreters then either overlook the reference to women who may have been deacons (1 Tim. 3:11) or insist that this does not refer to an authoritative or teaching office.

In 1 Timothy 2:15, Paul is often interpreted as offering some encouragement or consolation to women after limiting their role. It is suggested that he is intimating that motherhood is an honourable and proper role for women, or referring to the fact that the Messiah was born of a woman.

Other, more egalitarian, interpreters regard the prohibition against teaching or having authority over men as limited to the particular church situation in Ephesus and forbidding only *false* teaching. Heretical teaching is a major preoccupation of this letter; false teachers were plaguing the church in Ephesus 'with myths and endless genealogies'.[38] The false teaching does appear to have focused on women. From the letter it seems that women were being deluded and bringing the church into disrepute; possibly they were involved in sexual immorality.[39] This would account for Paul's emphasis on the need for women to dress and behave with propriety (1 Tim. 2:9, 15). The group may have involved women who 'want to be teachers of the law, but they do not know what they are talking about or what they so confidently affirm' (1 Tim. 1:7). This would explain why Paul encouraged women to *learn*, emphasizing that 'A woman should learn in quietness and full submission' (1 Tim. 2:11). A problem with this interpretation is that the verb *didaskō* ('teach') is usually used in connection with *sound* teaching. If Paul has false teaching in mind, why is he not more specific?

We can only speculate about the precise nature of the heresy. It could be that women within the church were imitating the immorality and teaching of the female-dominated fertility cults; after all, Ephesus was home of the goddess Artemis.[40] It has also been suggested that incipient gnosticism, teaching that Eve preceded Adam and procreated without male assistance, may have begun to influence the church in Ephesus. *Authentein*, usually translated 'have authority', is, as we have already mentioned, an extremely uncommon verb. It is possible that it could be translated 'begin something', 'take the initiative' or 'be primarily responsible for an action' (especially murder), 'rule', 'dominate', 'usurp power or rights' or even 'claim ownership, sovereignty or authorship'. Many have

173

interpreted *authentein* to mean that women should not use authority wrongly and teach error. But Catherine Kroeger suggests that if it is better translated as 'claim authorship', 1 Timothy 2:12 would then read, 'I do not allow a woman to teach nor to represent herself as the originator or source of man.'[41] Paul may have been prohibiting women from teaching myths similar to those of the gnostics, in which Eve was Adam's creator and Adam was deceived; in that case the emphasis on Adam as first-formed and not deceived is understandable (1 Tim. 2:13–14). Verse 15 too could be a response to a gnostic-type heresy which forbade childbearing and marriage. From this letter we know that there were heretics in Ephesus who 'forbid people to marry' (1 Tim. 4:3). If, however, reference to Eve's deception does not refer to the content of the false teaching, it may simply be a warning similar to the one in 2 Corinthians 11:3 that women are in danger of being deceived by heresy as Eve was.

A third interpretation limits the prohibition against teaching and exercising authority to wives who were teaching their husbands. It is argued that this accounts for the change in verse 11 from the plural to the singular, and for the reference to creation.[42] It may also explain why Paul refers to motherhood (verse 15). Generally, however, Paul is more precise when talking about a marriage relationship and uses the possessive pronoun. The whole context of 1 Timothy 2 suggests a public church situation.

A fourth interpretation sees part of Paul's injunction as an absolute with universal application, and part as a temporary, cultural expression.[43] Female submission to male authority, it is said, is unchanging because it is rooted in creation. But female silence or quietness before male teaching is a first-century cultural expression of the male–female relationship, on a par with the reference to head coverings in 1 Corinthians 11. According to this interpretation, a woman may teach as long as she does not infringe the principle of headship. This interpretation develops the two antitheses in 1 Timothy 2 between 'silence' and 'teaching' on the one hand and 'submission' and 'authority' on the other. The value of this interpretation is that it may explain why Paul bases his argument on both Genesis 2 (God's original purpose) and Genesis 3 (the imperfect situation after the fall).

It is difficult to be totally convinced by any of these interpretations of 1 Timothy 2. The passage is too enigmatic for anyone to be dogmatic. Whichever interpretation one adopts, Paul's apparent restrictions on women must be meshed with the practice of the early church. Let us briefly survey the New Testament evidence for women's positive involvement in the New Testament church. Priscilla, who with her husband Aquila, explained the way of God more accurately to the learned Apollos (Acts 18:26), is described as Paul's 'fellow-worker' (Rom. 16:3). Similarly, Euodia and Syntyche are mentioned as contending at Paul's side in the cause of the gospel along with the rest of his fellow-workers (Phil. 4:3–4). The contribution of these women was obviously very significant and these references imply that they verbally explained the gospel. Mary worked hard in the church in Rome, and Persis, Tryphena and Tryphosa worked hard in the Lord (Rom. 16:6, 12). Phoebe was prominent in the church at Cenchrea where she functioned as a *diakonos* (deacon). She is also described as a *prostasis*, a helper, representative or one who stands before.[44] It may have been the case that some women operated as deaconesses.[45] Widows may have had a special role in prayer and practical ministry (1 Tim. 5:5, 9–10). There may also be a reference to a female apostle or a woman who was well known among the apostles in the greeting to Junia(s) in Romans 16:7.[46]

Paul mentions women's activities in passing in his letters. He does not give precise job descriptions along with the terms he uses – 'fellow-worker', 'deacon' or 'helper'. But he clearly regards it as quite acceptable that women should fulfil these roles. It is interesting that in 1 Corinthians 16:16 he uses the word usually translated 'fellow-worker' when he tells the church to 'submit to such as these and to everyone who joins in the work, and labours at it'.

Women also prophesied in the early church. Philip the evangelist had four unmarried daughters who prophesied, and women prophesied in the church in Corinth.[47] This is significant because in the same letter in which Paul mentions women prophesying he writes: 'In the church God has appointed first of all apostles, second prophets, third teachers . . . ' (1 Cor. 12:28). In this list prophecy seems to be valued more highly than teaching. Prophecy was the highest gift to which believers could aspire. He teaches the Corinthians to 'follow the way of love and eagerly desire spiritual gifts, especially the gift of prophecy' (1 Cor. 14:1). This raises a host of questions about the function of prophetesses in the New Testament. What exactly did these women do? Did their prophecies reveal future events and special knowledge,[48] or does prophecy overlap with inspired preaching and teaching? In what way were the words of the prophetesses authoritative?

According to Paul, prophecy is the declaration of a revelation from God (1 Cor. 14:29–33).[49] This may have involved revealing the secrets of the heart (1 Cor. 14:24–25), or future events (Acts 11:27–30; 21:11), or the gifts of an individual in the congregation (1 Tim. 1:18; 4:14). It may also include revelation of doctrinal 'mysteries' (1 Cor. 13:2).[50] Prophecy is given for the 'strengthening, encouragement and comfort' of the church so that 'everyone may be instructed and encouraged'.[51] The purpose of preaching is to 'correct, rebuke and encourage – with great patience and careful instruction' (2 Tim. 4:2). This suggests that although they are not identical, preaching and prophecy may overlap.[52] There seems no reason to believe that inspired prophecy is less authoritative than preaching or teaching.[53] Some would conclude that if women could 'prophesy' in Corinth, it is difficult to see why they may not 'preach' in our pulpits.[54]

When we come to the question of the authority of prophecy, we have to make a distinction between two types of prophecy. On the one hand, we have the words spoken by the Old Testament prophets and some New Testament prophets which have been recorded in Scripture. As such they are totally authoritative. On the other hand we find mention of the gift of prophecy which has to be carefully evaluated.[55] Paul told the church to weigh carefully and judge such prophecy (1 Cor. 14:29). It was not immediately accepted in the early church as having divine authority. The prophecy which is described in the New Testament had a limited authority;[56] nevertheless, once accepted as being genuine, it was taken to be authoritative. Agabus, for instance, predicted Paul's arrest in Jerusalem; the response of the distraught believers was, 'The Lord's will be done' (Acts 21:10–14). Paul reminds Timothy of the prophecies made about him and says, 'Do not neglect your gift, which was given you through a prophetic message' (1 Tim. 1:18; 4:14). Prophecy, once it had been evaluated, was believed and acted upon. It clearly carried authority. This must mean that the words of the prophetesses were in some sense authoritative.

What does all of this mean in practice? Which responsibilities can women undertake in the church? Which church offices may they occupy? Should women be ordained? These questions generate fierce debate. Ordination is the most thorny issue. There were no women among the twelve apostles; the New Testament does not mention female overseers or elders, but it does speak of women deacons, fellow-workers and prophetesses. Should the church, therefore, ordain women? This is not an easy question to answer because ordination in our different church traditions today bears little resemblance to its New Testament precedent. Modern church structures are very complex. In the Orthodox and Catholic traditions, at one end of the spectrum, ordination means consecration to a sacramental priesthood. In the Reformed traditions, by contrast, ordination means a commissioning to the office of pastor and teacher.

In many denominations the only option for a local church is to have one man (or one woman) as the minister or pastor – a situation that is less than ideal from a biblical point of view. The New Testament has little evidence of a one-person ministry. Paul seems to have appointed a group of elders in every church, and in some cases there were also deacons.[57] Among the deacons there were probably women.[58] Team ministry in which women play a part seems to be the New Testament pattern. Phoebe in particular seems to provide a precedent in being commissioned for a particular task in the church at Cenchrea (Rom. 16:1). If ordination means recognizing a woman's gifts, and commissioning her for a task in a team ministry where she is not the sole authority, there seems to be no reason why she may not be ordained.[59]

If the church has a sin of omission it is not so much that it has failed to ordain women but that it has failed to employ women's gifts. This is a far more important issue. Sadly, in the debate about ordination we can lose sight of the New Testament teaching about the priesthood of all believers and the church as the body of Christ composed of people with different gifts (1 Pet. 2:5). Christian women need every encouragement to use their gifts. Often our church structures discourage both men and women from developing their gifts. For too long we have approached the role of women in the church from the wrong angle, concentrating on what restrictions should be placed on them, while the real problem is how to encourage all believers to discover and use their gifts.

It is sad that when we think of Paul we automatically think of silence and submission and endless squabbles about difficult texts and tortuous Greek. We fail to see that Paul, like Jesus, affirmed women and that they are clearly visible in his ministry. Women were actively involved alongside men, as fellow-workers, in the task of spreading the good news of the gospel.

Notes

1 B. Friedan, *The Feminine Mystique* (Penguin, 1965), p. 77.

2 See *e.g.* P. Jewett, *Man as Male and Female* (Eerdmans, 1975), p. 142, and M. Langley, *Equal Woman* (Marshalls, 1983) p. 46.

3 On this interpretation see Jewett, *Man as Male and Female*, pp. 86–7.

4 W. M. Swartley, *Slavery, Sabbath, War and Women* (Herald Press, 1983), p. 186.

5 Swartley, *Slavery*, p. 186.

6 On possible interpretations see J. B. Hurley, *Man and Woman in Biblical Perspective* (IVP, 1981), pp. 168–71.

7 See M. Hayter, *The New Eve in Christ* (SPCK, 1987), pp. 124–6.

8 *Stromata* 3.18, quoted in M. Green, *To Corinth with Love* (Hodder and Stoughton, 1982), p. 159.

9 On this interpretation see M. J. Evans, *Woman in the Bible* (Paternoster, 1983), p. 102, and A. Kirk, 'Theology from a Feminist Perspective', in K. Keay (ed.), *Men, Women and God* (Marshall, Morgan and Scott, 1987), p. 39.

10 Gal. 5:22; Eph. 6:10.

11 *Diakonos* is used elsewhere for church officers (Phil. 1:1; 1 Tim. 3:8–13). For a discussion of the meaning of *prostatis* see Evans, *Woman in the Bible*, p. 125.

12 'Fellow-workers' is a term used for those who worked alongside Paul, *e.g.* Rom. 16:21; Col. 4:11.

13 Acts 18; Rom. 16:3–4.

14 1 Cor. 11:3–16; Eph. 5:21–33.

15 On the context of Gal. 3:28 see S. T. Foh, *Women and the Word of God* (Presbyterian and Reformed Publishing Co., 1979), pp. 140–1.

16 Quoted in S. B. Clark, *Man and Woman in Christ* (Servant Books, 1980), p. 293.

17 J. Stott, 'Man, Woman and the Bible', recorded lecture, London Institute of Contemporary Christianity.

18 On the understanding of *kephalē* in church history see R. A. Tucker, 'What Does Kephalē Mean in the New Testament?', Response, in A. Mickelsen (ed.), *Women, Authority and the Bible* (IVP, USA, 1986), pp. 111–8.

19 B. and A. Mickelsen, in Mickelsen (ed.), *Women, Authority and the Bible*, pp. 97–111.

20 Mickelsen (ed.), *Women, Authority and the Bible*, p. 109.

21 1 Cor. 11:3; Eph. 1:22; 4:15; 5:22–24; Col. 1:18; 2:10, 18–19.

22 J. Stott, *The Message of Ephesians* (IVP, 1984), p. 232.

23 1 Cor. 11:3; Eph. 5:24.

24 See Evans, *Woman in the Bible*, p. 75.

25 Evans, *Woman in the Bible*, p. 67.

26 1 Tim. 5:14; Tit. 2:4–5.

27 Eph. 6:4; 1 Tim. 3:4.

28 D. Spender, *Man-Made Language* (Routledge and Kegan Paul,

1980), pp. 42–3.

29 Quoted in Foh, *Women and the Word*, p. 117.

30 For a fuller discussion of the implausibility of this interpretation see Foh, *Women and the Word*, pp. 118–9.

31 This interpretation is summarized in Swartley, *Slavery*, p. 173.

32 On possible meanings of *lalein* see Foh, *Women and the Word*, pp. 120–1.

33 This interpretation is supported by Hurley, *Man and Woman*, pp. 188–9.

34 On 1 Cor. 14:34–36 as a prohibition to wives see Evans, *Woman in the Bible*, p. 100.

35 Interpretation suggested by A. Kirk, 'Theology from a Feminist Perspective', in Keay (ed.), *Men, Women and God*, pp. 36–7.

36 D. Spender, *Women of Ideas (and What Men have Done to Them)* (Ark: 1982), pp. 349–50.

37 On this interpretation see Foh, *Women and the Word*, pp. 122–3, and Hurley, *Man and Woman*, pp. 197–8.

38 1 Tim. 1:3–4; see also 1:18–20; 4:1–8; 5:16; 6:3–10.

39 1 Tim. 4:7; 5:11–15; 2 Tim. 3:6–7.

40 This interpretation is favoured by Michael Green, *To Corinth*, p. 159.

41 C. C. Kroeger, '1 Timothy 2:12 – A Classicist's View', in Mickelsen (ed.), *Women, Authority and the Bible*, p. 232.

42 This interpretation is suggested by Kirk, 'Theology from a Feminist Perspective', in Keay (ed.), *Men, Women and God*, p. 37.

43 See J. Stott, *Issues Facing Christians Today* (Marshalls, 1984), p. 252.

44 On meanings of *prostasis* see Evans, *Woman in the Bible*, pp. 125–6.

45 1 Tim. 3:11 NIV mg. For argumentation in favour of this interpretation see Foh, *Women and the Word*, pp. 95–6.

46 See Evans, *Woman in the Bible*, p. 124.

47 Acts 21:8–9; 1 Cor. 11:5.

48 Acts 11:27–30; 21:11; 1 Cor. 14:24–25.

49 On the essential characteristics of prophecy and the difference between prophecy and teaching see W. A. Grudem, *The Gift of Prophecy in 1 Corinthians* (University Press of America, 1982), pp. 139–40.

50 Grudem, *Gift of Prophecy*, pp. 177–8.

51 1 Cor. 14:3, 31; Acts 15:32.

52 On the relation between prophecy and preaching see G. Houston, *Prophecy Now* (IVP, 1989), pp. 84–5.

53 See I. H. Marshall, 'The Role of Women in the Church', in S. Lees (ed.), *The Role of Women* (IVP, 1984), pp. 189–90.

54 See Marshall, 'The Role of Women', in Lees (ed.), *The Role of*

Women, though both Grudem and Houston take the opposite view.

55 On the judging of prophecy see Grudem, *Gift of Prophecy*, pp. 62–7.

56 On the authority of prophecy see Grudem, *Gift of Prophecy*, pp. 7–10.

57 Acts 14:23; 20:17; Phil. 1:1; Tit. 1:5.

58 Rom. 16:1; 1 Tim. 3:11 NIV mg.

59 On women in ministry see Stott, *Message of Ephesians*, pp. 249–50.

Good news for women

WE began this book by looking at Cranach's painting in which God is depicted as male and Satan as female. Images like this, and interpretations in this vein, have added layer upon layer to the biblical account. For centuries, women have been pronounced unequal to men. But the Bible decrees just the opposite. It never suggests that God favours one sex more than the other.

According to Genesis, both sexes were made in God's image, to relate personally to God. Woman shared the same place as man in the created order, and the same purpose on earth. They were given joint responsibility for bearing children and for caring for the rest of creation. They were counterparts, companions and partners. Together they rebelled against God. They were found equally guilty and punished by hard labour, death, and exile from God's presence.

This is when their problems began. Life outside Eden was hard. Men and women were alienated from God and from each other. The Old Testament graphically describes the violence, deceit, oppression, hatred and manipulation that ensued. At the same time a theme of hope runs through biblical history. God repeatedly renewed a promise of deliverance. This came to fruition in Jesus.

The gospel is for male and female; Jesus made no distinction. He revealed himself to women as well as to men as the promised Messiah who would die on their behalf to cancel their debt of sin. He offers forgiveness to all who believe in him. Women along with men were included in his ministry and joined his followers. Jesus' disciples found his attitude to women disquieting. They were surprised to find him talking alone with an unclean woman, and were indignant when Jesus allowed a woman to anoint him.[1] They even tried to prevent women and children from coming to Jesus, but he overruled them (Mt. 15:21–28; 19:13–14). Women had never encountered a man like Jesus. They could bring their deepest needs to him. Women from different social backgrounds, from within Israel, from the surrounding nations, clean and unclean, sat at his feet, listened to his teaching, were healed and forgiven, and took to the road to follow him. This total inclusion of women continued in the early church as both men and women were empowered by the Holy Spirit to spread the good news of the gospel.

In spite of Jesus' affirmation of women, some still suspect that the gospel is not good news for them. A common objection is that, while Jesus was essentially a good man, kind to women and children and more enlightened than his contemporaries, it is the same old story, a man forgiving women.

This criticism misconstrues Jesus. As we have already seen, he proclaimed a non-sexist gospel. Salvation and forgiveness are for all who believe, men as well as women.

We cannot brush Jesus aside by saying that he was a 'good man'. He claimed to be much more. He revealed to the Samaritan woman that he was the Messiah, forgave the sins of the woman who washed his feet, and told Martha that he had power over death.[2] This is not the behaviour of a 'good man'. His contemporaries hurled stones at him for making such claims.[3] As C. S. Lewis pointed out, either he was a madman, or a liar who deliberately misled people, or he was God.[4] His life and resurrection from the dead bear out his claim to be God. The miracle is not only that Jesus was free of sexism but that he was completely free of sin. Jesus' treatment of women is one aspect of his perfect life. The only logical response to Jesus is to follow the example of so many women in the gospels; to repent and follow him.

In every way, the gospel is good news for women. It is not a man-made solution to our problems, or a man-made message. I once asked a woman who was disillusioned with Christianity, 'What would God have to do to convince you?' She replied without hesitation, 'Come to earth and show us the way out of this mess.'

This is of course exactly what Jesus has done. As God in the flesh, Jesus shows us not only how men and women can be reconciled and live in harmony, but how they can be reconciled and live at peace with God.

Notes

1 Jn. 4:4–26; Mt. 26:6–13.
2 Jn. 4:1–42; Lk. 7:40–50; Jn. 11:17–27.
3 Jn. 8:48–59; 10:22–39.
4 C. S. Lewis, *Mere Christianity* (Fontana, 1955), pp. 52–3.

Select bibliography

Blocher, Henri, *In the Beginning* (IVP, 1984). Deals with the first three chapters of Genesis.

Bloesch, Donald, *Is the Bible Sexist? Beyond Feminism and Patriarchalism* (Crossway, 1982).

Clark, Elizabeth, and Richardson, Herbert, *Women and Religion: A Feminist Sourcebook of Christian Thought* (Harper and Row, 1977).

Clark, Stephen B., *Man and Woman in Christ* (Servant Books, 1980). A thorough biblical exegesis; sections on church tradition written from a Catholic perspective.

Dowell, Susan, and Hurcombe, Linda, *Dispossessed Daughters of Eve* (SCM Press, 1980). Explores the impact of feminism on the church.

Evans, Mary J., *Woman in the Bible* (Paternoster Press, 1983). A thorough biblical exegesis from a moderate evangelical position.

Ferguson, George, *Signs and Symbols in Christian Art* (Oxford University Press, 1954).

Foh, Susan T., *Women and the Word of God* (Presbyterian and Reformed Publishing Co., 1979). Provides a Reformed perspective.

Hayter, Mary, *The New Eve in Christ: The Use and Abuse of the Bible in the Debate about Women in the Church* (SPCK, 1987).

Hebblethwaite, Margaret, *Motherhood and God* (Geoffrey Chapman, 1984).

Hurley, James, *Man and Woman in Biblical Perspective* (IVP, 1981). A careful exegesis combined with research into the cultural background.

Jewett, Paul H., *Man as Male and Female* (Eerdmans, 1975). A radical biblical feminist approach emphasizing cultural influences on the text.

Keay, Kathy (ed.), *Men, Women and God* (Marshall Pickering, 1987). Evangelicals on feminist issues.

Knight, George W., *The New Testament Teaching on the Role Relationship of Men and Women* (Baker, 1977). A traditional approach.

Langley, Myrtle S., *Equal Woman: A Christian Feminist Perspective* (Marshall, Morgan and Scott, 1983). A radical biblical feminist approach similar to Jewett's.

Lees, Shirley (ed.), *The Role of Women* (IVP, 1984). Eight evangelical Christians debate.

Lewis, Alan E. (ed.), *The Motherhood of God* (St Andrew Press, 1984). A summary of biblical and historical material.

Maitland, Sara, *A Map of the New Country – Women and Christianity* (Routledge and Kegan Paul, 1975). A revisionist approach which explores many different facets of Christian feminism.

Marquet, Claudette, *Femme et homme il les créa* (Les Bergers et les Mages, 1984). Written from the perspective of a pastor in the French Reformed Church.

Mickelsen, Alvera (ed.), *Women, Authority and the Bible* (IVP, USA, 1986). A compilation of twenty-six evangelicals.

Mollenkott, Virginia Ramey, *Women, Men and the Bible* (Abingdon, 1977). A radical biblical feminist approach.

Moltmann-Wendel, Elisabeth, *The Women Around Jesus* (SCM Press, 1982).

O'Faolain, Julia, and Martines, Lauro (eds.), *Not in God's Image: Women in History* (Virago, 1979).

Phillips, John A., *Eve: The History of an Idea* (Harper and Row, 1984). The history of Eve in Western civilizations.

Richards, Janet Radcliffe, *The Sceptical Feminist: A Philosophical Enquiry* (Pelican, 1982).

Rotelle, John E., *Mary's Yes from Age to Age: Readings on Mary through the Ages* (Collins, 1989).

Ruether, Rosemary Radford, *Mary – The Feminine Face of the Church* (SCM Press, 1979).

Ruether, Rosemary Radford, *New Woman, New Earth* (Seabury, 1975). A revisionist approach.

Ruether, Rosemary Radford (ed.), *Religion and Sexism: Images of Woman in the Jewish and Christian Traditions* (Simon and Schuster, 1974).

Russell, Letty M. (ed.), *Feminist Interpretations of the Bible* (Basil Blackwell, 1985). Contributions by leading revisionist feminists.

Scanzoni, Letha, and Hardesty, Nancy, *All We're Meant to Be: A Biblical Approach to Women's Liberation* (Word Books, 1974). A biblical feminist approach.

186

Spender, Dale, *Women of Ideas (and What Men have Done to Them)* (Ark, 1982). A feminist history.

Stanton, Elizabeth Cady (ed.), *The Woman's Bible: the Original Feminist Attack on the Bible* (1895: Polygon, 1985).

Storkey, Elaine, *What's Right with Feminism* (SPCK, 1985). Explores shades of feminist thinking, the feminist case against the church and a Christian feminist response.

Stott, John, *Issues Facing Christians Today* (Marshalls, 1984). Includes a section on women, men and God from a moderate evangelical perspective.

Swartley, William M., *Slavery, Sabbath, War and Women* (Herald Press, 1983). Case studies in biblical interpretation.

Trible, Phyllis, *God and the Rhetoric of Sexuality* (Fortress, 1978). A moderate revisionist author.

Warner, Marina, *Alone of All her Sex: The Myth and Cult of the Virgin Mary* (Picador, 1976). A historical exploration of the virgin's cult in Western cultures.

Index